A Road Guide To
DELHI

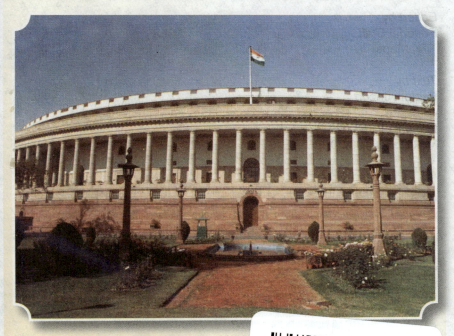

TTK Healthcare Limited - Publications Division

© TTK Healthcare Limited – Publications Division, 2010
Statutory declaration under Section 52A of the Indian Copyright Act, 1957.

All rights reserved. No part of this book or map may be reproduced, stored in a retrieval system or transmitted in any form or by any means – electronic, mechanical, photocopying, recording or otherwise – without prior written permission from TTK Healthcare Limited – Publications Division. Brief text quotations, with use of photographs are exempted for purpose of book reviews only.

Great care has been taken in the compilation, updation, validation and generation of the cartographic data. However, as various sources have been referred, the publishers are not responsible for errors, if any, and their consequences.

Edited by:
Editorial Staff,
TTK Maps

Text by:
Fabiola Jacob

ISBN 81 7053 020 2
M.R.P.: Rs.100.00

Designed, compiled, cartographed, typeset, and published by
TTK Healthcare Limited - Publications Division
Plot No.13, 1st Avenue, Mahindra World City, Natham Sub Post, Chengalpet (Taluk), Kanchipuram (District) 603 002. India.
Tel : 044-47425050 - 99, Fax : 044-47425051
E-mail : support@ttkmaps.com
Visit us at : www.ttkmaps.com

Printed at :
Canara Traders & Printers Pvt. Ltd., Chennai - 600 041.

Disclaimer: Great care has been taken in the compilation of data for this guidebook and map, to make it useful and informative. And to this end, information has been sourced from various means such as tourist booklets, guidebooks and the Internet. Should there be any discrepancy in the information provided, the Publishers are not liable for their consequences, if any.

And please note, certain places mentioned in the text may not be marked on the map, due to lack of authentic information or lack of space in the map.

Telephone numbers and addresses are likely to change from time to time. In case of any difficulty, please refer the local telephone directory or a dial-in enquiry service.

We make no warranty about the accuracy or completeness of contents. And we disclaim all liability arising from its use.

CONTENTS

- DELHI 4
  - HISTORY 4
  - GEOGRAPHY 6
  - FESTIVALS AND SPECIAL EVENTS 6
  - SHOPPING 8
  - HOW TO GET THERE 8
- DELHI AREA MAP 17
- WHAT TO SEE 10
  - GARDENS & PARKS 13
  - MONUMENTS AND MEMORIALS 71
  - MUSEUMS AND ART GALLERIES 76
- EXCURSIONS 79
- EATING OUT 81
  - RESTAURANTS 83
  - FAST FOOD 85
- ENTERTAINMENT 86
  - SHOPPING MALLS 86
  - CINEMA HALLS 87
  - ART GALLERIES 87
  - BAR & PUBS 88
- GETTING AROUND THE CITY 88
  - CALL TAXIS 88
  - 24 HOURS TAXI SERVICES 88
  - CAR RENTALS 89
  - IMPORTANT BUS ROUTES 89
  - TOURIST BUS SERVICES 92
  - DELHI METRO RAILWAY 92
  - TOURIST INFORMATION CENTERS 93
  - OTHER STATE TOURISM OFFICES 93
  - AIR LINES 94
- ESSENTIAL SERVICES 95
  - BANKS 95
  - ATMS 96
  - FOREIGN MONEY EXCHANGE 96
  - CONSULATES AND EMBASSIES 97
  - EMERGENCY PHONE NUMBERS 98
- HEALTHCARE 99
  - HOSPITALS 99
  - BLOOD BANKS 99
  - AMBULANCE SERVICES 99
  - 24-HOUR PHARMACIES 99
- ACCOMMODATION 100

DELHI

India Gate

"Here we stand in Delhi, symbol of old and new ... the grace of many empires and the nursery of a republic" – Jawaharlal Nehru, the first Prime Minister of India, summed up the essence of Delhi thus. Decades later, Delhi, the seat of one of the World's largest democracies, has proved itself as a truly cosmopolitan city. Delhi is today, one of the most elegant capitals in the world. Here one can see the mingling of many cultures, languages, traditions and peoples into one united nation.

Delhi City, the showcase of India, has been the centre of political activity from time immemorial. The ancient fortresses, majestic buildings and historic ruins find their modern counterparts in the tall skyscrapers, diplomatic enclaves and well-planned townships of New Delhi. The people here, their lifestyles, traditions and even the climate are a rich and varied mixture of all that is Indian. Delhi welcomes both the pleasure-seeker and the mystic. "Lose yourself in Delhi" says Khushwant Singh, for "You may find its soul – and your own".

HISTORY

The early history of Delhi, is an interesting mixture of myth and reality. The strategic location of Delhi, between the Aravalli hills and the river Yamuna, had attracted the attention of almost every king or conqueror in this part of the world. The earliest reference to Delhi as a settlement is made in the Hindu epic, Mahabharata which states that the Pandavas founded a city called Indraprashta, beside the river Yamuna in 1450 BC.

Ever since then, conquerors from the north treated Delhi as a gateway to the Indian sub-continent. With repeated invasions and successions of empires and kingdoms, Delhi was established and demolished time and again. Each dynasty built a new city, which reflected on the times and lifestyles of the ruler. Thus, in the course of history, seven medieval cities were formed.

The first city of Delhi was built by the Tomar King Anangpal in 1069 A.D. It was further improved by his successors, Prithviraj Chauhan, the famous Rajput warrior and Qutb-ud-din Aibak, the first Muslim Sultan of Delhi. Qutb-ud-din Aibak began the construction of the Qutab Minar, which still dominates the landscape of Delhi. Alauddin Khilji, one of the greatest sultans, built a magnificent new city Siri, in the 11th century. This prosperous city, located northeast of the original Tomar township, came to be the second medieval city of Delhi.

When Ghiyyassudin Tughlak seized power in 1320, he built the third city of Delhi – Tughlakabad, in the hills of south Delhi, a few miles east of the Qutab Minar. But Tughlakabad was inhabited for only five years as Ghiyasuddin's son and successor, Sultan Muhammad Tughlak built Jahanpanah, Delhi's fourth city between Lalkot and Siri. In 1327, Muhammad Shah, a brilliant but eccentric ruler transferred the capital from Delhi to Daulatabad in the Deccan. The move was ultimately a failure and Delhi resumed the status of the capital once again.

Delhi experienced an era of peace and prosperity, with the accession of Feroz Shah Tughlak in 1351. Ferozabad, the fifth city of Delhi was built by him along the banks of the river Yamuna. Feroz Shah was a great builder and so, this fifth city of Delhi was full of splendid palaces, mosques and gardens.

After the historic battle of Panipat in 1526, Babur, the first great Mughal, invaded India and set himself up as the ruler of Hindustan. His son and successor Humayun, started building the Mughal capital of Dinapanah during his reign. But by 1540, Sher Shah Suri, the Afghan invader, drove Humayun out of Delhi and built a mighty empire with the best administrative system that the city had ever seen. This sixth city, Shergarh, extended north from the Purana Qila, to the edge of Feroz Shah Kotla. In 1555, Humayun regained the kingdom of Delhi, and once again the capital passed into the hands of the Mughals. Under the flourishing rule of Akbar, the kingdom was further extended and Agra became the centre of activity. Many important monuments – namely, the Red Fort and Taj Mahal were built there during the reign of Shah Jahan. But, in 1638, Shah Jahan decided to shift the capital to Delhi and so by 1648, Shahjahanabad, the seventh city of Delhi was built. Many monuments of Shahjahanabad remain even today and they now form a part of Old Delhi.

The Decline of the Mughal Empire started during the reign of Aurangzeb, and by the end of the 18th century, Delhi became a pale shadow of its former self. The 19th century saw the British East India company rise in power, as Bahadur Shah Zafar, the last of the Mughals, surrendered to the British, thereby paving the way for a new dynasty in Delhi. But under the British Raj, Delhi was only of secondary importance as Calcutta was the capital of British India. But finally, in the spectacular Coronation

Durbar in 1911, King George V formally announced the transfer of the British Indian capital to Delhi. The famous British architects Sir Edward Lutyens and Sir Herbert Baker were given the task of designing New Delhi, the eighth city of Delhi. Raisina Hill was chosen as the pivotal point and the Rashtrapati Bhavan along with the administrative headquarters was built here. In January 1931, New Delhi was inaugurated as the imperial capital of the British Raj, and it has endured to this day, as the capital of the Indian Union.

GEOGRAPHY

The Union territory of Delhi, is located at an altitude of 239m above sea level in the middle of the Great North Indian plain. Spread over an area of 1500 sq km, Delhi and its suburbs have a population of over 9 million. Delhi City is surrounded by Uttar Pradesh on the East and Haryana on the West. The rocky ridges on the northwest frontiers act as natural barriers of the city. The Yamuna, the second-most sacred river in India, flows through the eastern part of Delhi. The great plains of northern India, are located to the south of Delhi city.

The climate of Delhi is always in extremes because of its exposure to the plains. Delhi summers are unbearably hot, as hot winds and dust storms make the mercury shoot up. The best season to visit Delhi is soon after the Monsoon as the rains help reduce the sweltering heat and prepare the city for winter. Winter in Delhi, is bitterly cold, but the city adorns a unique charm in this season. Flower gardens with chrysanthemums and roses in full bloom, the Red Fort on a cold winter morning, army men in crisp uniforms marching down Rajpath on a misty republic day and a walk down Mughal gardens on a foggy evening, are some of the many delights that Delhi winter has to offer.

SEASONS	MONTHS
Winter / Spring	November-March
Summer	April-June
Monsoon	July-September

FESTIVALS AND SPECIAL EVENTS

Delhi's social calendar is filled with exciting events throughout the year. Both summer and winter in Delhi have their share of religious festivals and cultural extravaganza. The year begins with the festival of **Lori** in January, which marks the height of winter. This mid-winter festival is celebrated by burning bonfires and singing and dancing.

The **Republic Day Parade** celebrated on January 26th, is Delhi's most spectacular pageant. Smartly dressed soldiers, bands and school children march briskly down Rajpath as the President of India takes the salute. Tableaux depicting unique features of the Indian States, folk dancers and caparisoned elephants form a part of this colourful pageant.

Two days after the Republic day parade, the **Beating Retreat** is held at Vijay Chowk. Camels silhouetted against Rashtrapati Bhavan at dusk, with army men marching to the band music, present a truly spectacular sight.

The **Garden Festival** in February is a celebration of the city's many spectacular gardens that burst into a riot of colour, especially in winter. It is an ideal meeting point for gardening enthusiasts.

The festival of **Holi** in March, which hails the arrival of spring, is celebrated all over Delhi with great festivity. Men and women throw colour on each other and sing and dance during this joyous occasion. Another festival typical of Delhi is **Phoolwalon Ki Sair**, the festival of flower sellers. On this day, flower sellers present colourful flower fans to the Gods, and pray for a better flower-reason in the coming year.

October brings the **Dussehra**, a major Indian festival, when scenes from the epic Ramayana are enacted in various parts of the city. Dussehra is followed by **Diwali**, the festival of lights, which is celebrated all over the country with pomp and grandeur. Most homes are illuminated with oil lamps, and the sound and light of firecrackers can be seen and heard throughout the city.

The **Qutab Festival of Classical Music and Dance** is organised by Delhi Tourism in October at the Qutab Minar complex.

All religious festivals are celebrated among the respective communities, with a distinct regional flavour.

Winter has its own share of events, as the city bursts into bloom in November – December. **Christmas** too is celebrated in Delhi, and special services are held in Churches. The **Delhi Horse Show**, outside the walls of the Red fort, the **Vintage Car Rally**, the **Rose Show**, **Chrysanthemum Show** and the **Delhi Flower Show** held during the winter months, add to the charm of the season.

Dussehra Festival

SHOPPING

Delhi is a shopper's paradise. There are wares here to suit all purses and bargaining is the order of the day. Delhi's main shopping centres are Connaught Place, Chandni Chouk and Karol Bagh, which are known for their variety of shops ranging from doric-columned arcades, air-conditioned under ground markets (like Palika Bazaar) and little shops crammed along winding medieval streets.

Delhi markets sell a wide variety of goods ranging from designer garments to antique pieces. Following is a list of some of the shopping centres and their speciality items.

Ajmal Khan Market	– Textiles, Crockery, trinkets, dry fruits and spices
Bhagirath Place	– Electronic goods
Chandni Chouk	– Rare antiques, traditional sweets
Chawri Bazaar	– Antique copper and brassware
Connaught Place	– Textiles, leather goods and traditional ware
Dariba Kalan	– Traditional silverware
Kinari Bazaar	– Silk sarees
Palika Bazaar	– Textiles & electrical goods
Punchkuin Bazaar	– Furniture
Raja Garden	– Marble
Sunder Nagar Market	– Paintings and antique jewellery
Sadar Bazaar	– Wholesale market

CLOSED DAYS FOR SHOPPING CENTRES

Sunday: Connaught Place, Janpath, Babu Kharak Singh Marg, Shankar Market, Punchkuin Road, Jor Bach, Khan Market, Nehru Place, Sunder Nagar, Yashwant Place, Chandni Chouk, Hauz Khas Village.

Monday: Defence Colony, Karol Bagh, Jangpura, Lajpat Nagar, Nizamuddin, South Extension, INA.

Tuesday: Greater Kailash, Green Park, Hauz Khas, Safdarjung Enclave, Vasant Vihar, Yusuf Sarai, New Friends Colony, Chittaranjan Park.

Wednesday: West Delhi, Paschim Vihar, Rajouri Garden, Salimar Bagh, Tilak Nagar, Sarojini Nagar.

HOW TO GET THERE

By Air

Delhi is conveniently connected to all the major cities of the world with almost all the major airlines operating out of here. New Delhi has two airports catering to domestic and international flights, located 4½ km apart in Palam. The international airport (known as Indira Gandhi International Airport) is situated 20 km from the city center. Taxis and coaches are available from the airports.

By Rail
Delhi is connected to almost all the cities in the country by super-fast and express trains. The city has three major railway stations at New Delhi, Old New Delhi, and Nizamuddin. Luxury trains like the Palace-on-Wheels, Fairy Queen, and Royal Orient Express can be taken from New Delhi Safdarjung Railway Station. Rajdhani Express trains connect New Delhi from the state capitals. Shatabdi Express trains connect New Delhi to the neighboring cities.

It is wise to book tickets well in advance for trains are almost always crowded. Tickets can also be booked through travel agents.

By Road
Delhi is well connected by road to all major destinations in North India. The Inter State Bus Terminus (ISBT) are located at Kashmiri Gate, Sarai Kale-Khan and Anand Vihar. The Inter-State Bus Terminus at Kashmiri Gate is said to be the largest in Asia. Buses to all neighbouring states are available at frequent intervals.

Delhi is connected by a network of roads to all the major cities and towns of India. The Automobile Association of Upper India (AAUI) assists in arranging reservations at tourist rest houses, circuit houses or Dak bungalows run by government organisation.

PUBLIC TRANSPORT
Travelling in scheduled Delhi Transport Corporation (DTC) buses or privately-run mini-buses during peak hours can be a nightmarish experience for the uninitiated. It would be far safer to travel by the special buses and vans that the DTC operates.

Delhi Metro (counterpart of 'Subways' in the United States and 'Tubes' in London) is the latest marvel that Delhi boasts of. This is a clean, fast and comfortable mode of transportation. Delhi's suburban railway, called the Ring Railway, originates from the Nizamuddin Railway Station.

Scooter rickshaws and taxis abound in the capital. Rates are metered and they are, on the whole, reliable. The motorcycle rickshaw, a quaint vehicle that seats six, is still found in some parts of the city.

If one is tired of walking down the winding gullies and 'Kuchchas' of Old Delhi then the only other means of transportation is the cycle rickshaw.

The *tonga* (horse-drawn carriage) is an impractical mode of transport but it is nevertheless found in some parts of Old Delhi and near New Delhi Railway Station. A moonlight ride in this vehicle down Delhi's historic Civil Lines may however prove to be the ideal treat for the incurable romantic.

WHAT TO SEE

Azad Hind Gram Tourist Complex *(at National Highway No.10)*

Located at Tikri Kalan, within 2 kms. from the Delhi-Haryana border, this project was developed by Delhi Tourism to honour Nethaji Subhash Chandra Bose, a famous freedom fighter. While the buildings here are all in the traditional North Indian style, the village showcases the many traditions of Indian craftsmanship. The complex also has a museum and memorial, besides facilities for shopping plazas, an amphitheater, souvenir and garden shop, food kiosks, restaurants and convention hall.

Bahai's House of Worship

This gleaming white structure, shaped like a Lotus, is made of marble, cement, dolomite and sand. Located in Bahapur Hill, the Lotus temple is meant for the worship of God, irrespective of caste, creed, race or nation. Visitors are expected to maintain silence inside the temple premises. A visit to the Bahai temple is a must both for the tourists and those in search of peace and tranquility.

Bahai's House

Connaught Place

Delhi's premier shopping centre, Connaught Place is famed for the Handicrafts, curios, old paintings and wooden carvings that can be bought here. Connaught Place is also a centre of entertainment and commercial activity. Built in 1931, this complex is made up of two concentric circles of colonnaded buildings. The outer circle is referred to as Connaught Circus. Connaught Place is today, an interesting reminder of post-colonial India.

Birla Mandir

Dilli Haat

Dilli Haat is located in one of the most important commercial centers of South Delhi, opposite INA market. The word Haat refers to a weekly market in rural, semi-urban and sometimes even urban India. Dilli Haat is not just a market place; it has been visualized as a showpiece of traditional Indian culture- a forum where rural life and folk art are brought closer to an urban clientele.

Dilli Haat is home to nearly 50,000 handicraft and handloom artisans. The complex is not only artistic, but also recreational in nature where the entire family can have a good time and relish a wide variety of cuisine. Besides an International Food Plaza there are 25 stalls dishing out sumptuous delicacies from different States and Union Territories; an Exhibition Hall; a Souvenir shop selling an assortment of small gift items; an open stage for cultural programmes and a play area for children.

Jawaharlal Nehru Stadium

This giant open-air stadium on Lodi Road has an enormous audience capacity of 75,000. Well equipped with all the latest technological innovations, this international sports stadium is served by a network of fly-overs.

Lakshmi Narayan Temple (Birla Mandir)

Built by the eminent Industrialist Raja Baldev Birla in 1938, and inaugurated by Mahatma Gandhi, this popular shrine contains a large number of idols representing the various gods of the Indian pantheon. Located on Mandir Marg, the main deities in this temple are Narayana (the Preserver) and Lakshmi (the Goddess of Wealth). A *Dharmasthala* (rest house for pilgrims) is located near this temple.

Parliament House (Sansad Bhavan)

To the north of Rashtrapati Bhavan stands the Parliament House, a domed, circular structure measuring almost a kilometre in circumference. Designed by Lutyens, this colonnaded building contains the two houses

Rashtrapati Bhavan

of parliament (Lok Sabha and Rajya Sabha) and the Parliament Library. Tourists can gain access to the visitor's gallery by obtaining a special pass. The best time to visit would be when the parliament is in session.

To the left of Sansad Bhavan is the **Cathedral Church of the Redemption**, the Anglican Cathedral. Built by H.A.N. Medd in 1935, the Cathedral was constructed in the same imperial style as the Rashtrapati Bhavan.

Pragati Maidan

This sprawling exhibition ground on Mathura Road is the venue for the national and international trade fairs, which draw large crowds throughout the year. Many business and industrial organisations from all over the world participate in these fairs, which result in exchange of technical prowess, industrial collaboration and joint ventures. The Nehru Pavilion, Atomic Energy and Defence Pavilion are of considerable interest. The handcrafted skills of Indian artisans are on display at the Crafts Museum and the States Pavilion. The 7-acre village complex is also worth visiting.

Pragati Maidan also houses **Appu Garh** – a mini amusement park. The modern children's playground has some of the world's famous sophisticated equipment meant for children at play.

Timings: Week days: 9.30 am to 5.30 pm
           Sundays and Public Holidays: 9.30 am to 8.00 pm.

Rashtrapati Bhavan

This official residence of the President of India was formerly the Viceregal Palace. Designed by Lutyens, the palace and its gardens cover almost 330 acres. This 340-room palace on Raisina Hill, is a complex of great courts, pillared porticos, marble-lined vestibules, magnificent staterooms, majestic stairways, fountains and gardens. The magnificent Durbar hall, with its massive 8-m dome and marble walls is now used for formal ceremonies. The Ashoka Hall with its painted ceiling, the portraits of former viceroys in the dining hall and the impressive staterooms are truly a sight to behold. The palace overlooks the raised and terraced Mughal gardens on the west. Special permission has to be obtained in advance to visit the Rashtrapati Bhavan.

St. James Church

The oldest church in Delhi, St. James Church, was built by Colonel James Skinner, the son of a Scotsman and a Rajput lady. Consecrated in 1836, this fine Church was built in redemption of a pledge made on the battlefield when he lay dying. Built in Baroque style, this Anglican Church stands amidst an immaculate churchyard filled with flowering plants and graves of British settlers.

GARDENS & PARKS

Ajmal Khan Park

Spread over an area of five acres, the Ajmal Khan Park is an ideal getaway from the Capital's hustle and bustle. The **Musical Fountain** - its colourful lights synchronized with music and the cascading water - is the main attraction here. The Musical Fountain is switched on for two hours everyday after sunset, except on Tuesdays.

Buddha Jayanti Park

This garden, on Ridge road was laid out to commemorate the 2,500th anniversary of Lord Buddha's attainment of Nirvana. The sloping terrain of the Ridge have been converted into wooded areas, glades, rockeries, streams and bridges. The stone paths here lead to quiet, secluded corners that provide an atmosphere of peace and tranquility – ideal for meditation. The park also has a flourishing Bodhi tree, which was a sapling of the original tree of enlightenment. The park is rich in bird life and is a favourite jogging haunt among tourists and the residents of Delhi.

Bhagwan Mahavir Vanasthali

Laid out to commemorate the 2500th Nirvana anniversary of Lord Mahavir, this beautiful garden on Ridge Road is ideal for morning walks and meditation.

Deer Park

Situated in the Chankyapuri area and easily accessible from Hauz Khas Village and Safdarjung Enclave, the park has been beautifully landscaped with shady trees and lawns, and a tranquil water body.

Garden of Five Senses

Located at Said-Ul-Azaib village, close to the Mehrauli heritage area in New Delhi, this initiative by Delhi Tourism Transportation Development Corporation is not just a park, but a space with a variety of activities, inviting public interaction and exploration. Majestic rocks stand silhouetted against the sky, others lie strewn upon the ground in a casual yet alluring display of nature's sculptural genius. Its a public leisure space that is intended to awaken a sensory response and thereby a sensitivity to the environment.

Soaring stainless-steel birds mounted on slate-clad pillars welcome you into the park. An expansive plaza, set on the natural slope of the site, invites you up the spiral walkway. Across are a troop of elephants, cut in stone, regaling in a water bath.

The garden itself is divided into distinct areas. On one side of the spiral walkway is the Khas Bagh, a formal garden patterned on the lines of the Mughal Garden. Slow-moving water cascades in channels along its length, while flowering and fragrant shrubs and trees line its paths. The Central axis leads to a series of fountains, some of which are lit up by fibreoptic lighting systems. Encapsulating the expression here is the sculpture of 'A Fountain Tree". Secluded, away from the heart of the garden, on the other side of the walkway is the food and shopping court.

Jama-Masjid

Kalindi Kunj

Situated in South Delhi, Kalindi Kunj is famous for architecture coupled with greenery. It is a perfect place for evenings out with the family.

Lodi Gardens

Laid out by Lady Willingdon in 1930, this beautiful park contains the majestic domed tombs of several sultans. The blossoming shrubs, flowering trees, fountains, bushes and ponds serve as an ideal habitat for the wide variety of bird life found here. This park is a favourite haunt of early morning joggers and those in search of solitude.

Humayun's Tomb

Millennium Indraprasht Park

Located on the Outer Ring Road in East Delhi, India, near the Sarai Kale Khan Bus terminal, this park was constructed in 2004 by the Delhi Development Authority. The park has a children's park, an amphitheatre and a food court. A large World Peace Stupa called the Vishwa Shanti Stupa is being constructed in the park.

Mahatma Gandhi Park

Situated behind the Town Hall building on the main Church Mission Road, near Old Delhi Railway Station, this park is known more for its historical significance. It was originally set up during the British period and was officially known as "Queen's Park". However, amongst the masses, it came to be known as the "Company Bagh". In the early part of the 19th century, Company Bagh functioned as the outdoor club for Delhi's high-class society. It was renamed the Mahatma Gandhi Park, after India attained independence in the year 1947.

Today, the park has a number of trees that provide relief from the scorching heat of summer, along with a statue of Mahatma Gandhi and is an open-air space for the residents of the congested Chandni Chowk area. It also serves as the venue for various cultural and social activities during the festival season.

Mughal Gardens

Forming a part of the Rashtrapati Bhavan estate, Mughal Gardens is the venue of tea parties hosted by the President in honour of visiting dignitaries. Designed by Lutyens, the gardens is made up of green velvet lawns, sparkling fountains, terraces, flower beds and pathways that lead to a secret garden. Wide varieties of rose species can be found in the rose garden here. The ponds in Mughal Gardens contain many interesting varieties of fresh water fish and aquatic plants. The Mughal Gardens are open to the public in February and March.

National Zoological Park

The Delhi Zoo, one of the finest in Asia, was established in 1959, along the southwest wall of Purana Qila. Spread over an area of 214 acres, the Zoo was designed on an open plan, where the wild animals are provided with a natural habitat. Wide water channels serve as the only barrier between animals and visitors. The zoo houses more than 2,000 animals and birds from Asia, Africa, America and Australia. The collection also includes rare and endangered Indian species like tiger, panther, one-horned rhinoceros, gharial and white tiger. The Zoo is a bird-watcher's paradise in autumn, as several migratory birds visit the place. The beautifully landscaped grounds of the Zoo are ideal for a picnic.

Timings: Summer   : 8.00 am to 6.00 pm
              Winter : 9.00 am to 5.00 pm
Closed on Fridays

Nehru Park

This beautifully landscaped park in Chanakyapuri is filled with grassy mounds, ponds, groves, flowering trees and flowerbeds. The park also has a swimming pool and snack bar.

Netaji Subhash Park

Situated on Netaji Subhash Marg, opposite Sunehri Masjid in the old city, this is a rather small park adjoining the Urdu Park. The Netaji Subhash Park is quite famous for its *malishwallahs* (body masseurs). Infact, many people come here to get a body massage from the excellent masseurs here. The park also has an impressive statue of Netaji Subhash Chandra Bose.

Janatar Mantar

(Continued on page 71)

DELHI AREA MAPS

CONTENTS

Title	Page No.	Title	Page No.
Chanakyapuri	18 - 19	Janakpuri	36 - 37
India Gate	20 - 21	Qutb Institutional Area	38 - 39
Karol Bagh	22 - 23	Lajpat Nagar & Siri Area	40 - 41
Old Delhi	24 - 25	Tughlakabad	42 - 43
Rohini	26 - 27	Okhla	44 - 45
Model Town	28 - 29	Ghaziabad	46 - 47
Mustafabad & Shahdara	30 - 31	Faridabad	48 - 49
Rajendra Nagar	32 - 33	Gurgaon	50 - 51
Krishna Nagar	34 - 35	Noida	52 - 53

LEGEND

- **OKHLA** — Area Names
- *Lodi Road* — Road Names
- Airlines
- Apartments
- Auditorium
- Banks
- Bus Terminus
- Business Organisations
- Cinema
- Circles & Junctions
- Clubs / Membership Institutions
- Diplomatic Missions
- Educational Institutions
- Government Offices
- Historical Places
- Hospitals
- Hotels & Restaurants
- Miscellaneous
- Museums & Art Galleries

Places of Worship
- Temples
- Gurudwara
- Churches
- Mosques

- Police Stations
- Post Offices
- Railway Stations
- Shopping Centres
- Travel Agencies
- Wedding Halls

Chanakyapuri

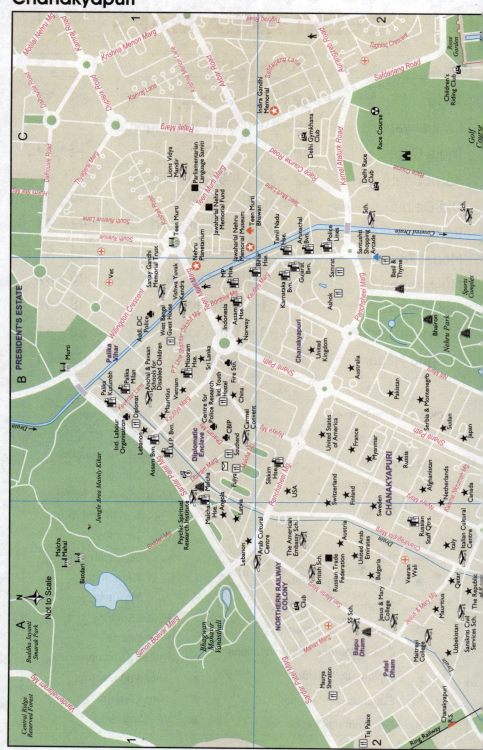

India Gate

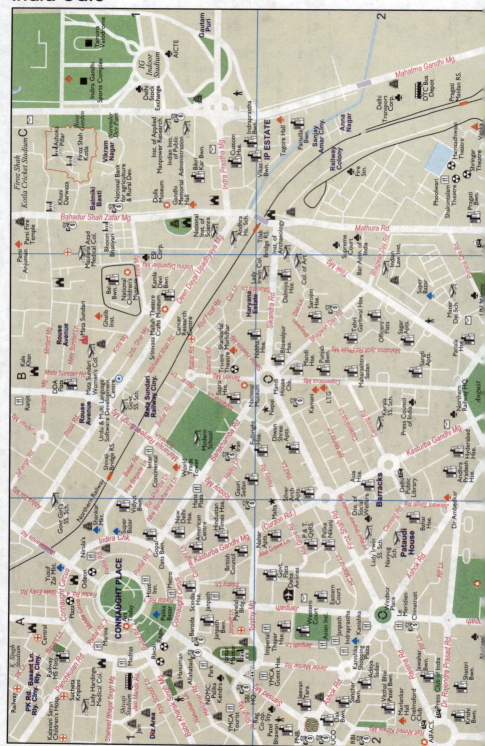

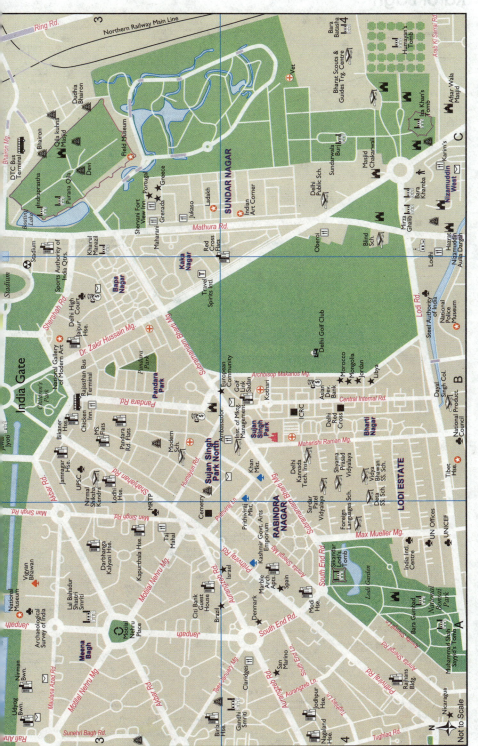

Karol Bagh

Map 23

C | **D**

Grid 1

- AZAD NAGAR
- Hindi Academy
- Sabzi Mandi RS.
- Sabzi Mandi
- Aram Ganj
- Palace
- Ice Factory
- Roshanara Rd.
- GT Rd.
- Kali Das Mg.
- Ram Bagh
- Motia Bagh Rly. Clny.
- Chandra Shekhar Azad Clny.
- Bhagat Singh Mg.
- Railway Qtrs.
- Old Rohtak Rd.
- Azad Market
- Ram Bagh Rd.
- Naya Mohalla
- Nawab Ganj
- Library Rd.
- Scouts & Trng. Centre
- Kishan Ganj
- Northern Railway Main Line
- Azad Market Rd.
- Kishan Ganj RS.
- SS Sch.
- Hathi Khana
- Fyaz Ganj
- DCM Rd.
- Bahadurgarh Rd.
- Railway Clny.
- Bara Hindu Rao
- Bara Hindu Rao Rd.
- Seng Tengala Bara Ganj

Grid 2

- KISHAN GANJ
- Saraswati Park
- Goushala Mg.
- Lady Reading Health Sch.
- Anaj Mandi
- Chowk Nai Basti
- DCM HS.Sch.
- Model Basti
- Filmistan
- Pahari Dhiraj
- SS Sch.
- Gali Gopal Wali
- Mandir Mg.
- Gauhar Rd.
- Govt SS Sch.
- Chamberlain Mg.
- SADAR BAZAR
- Tibbia Col.
- Tibbia
- Dori Walan
- Maharishi Balmiki Mg.
- Nawab Rd.
- Jameel Hostel
- Brahma Kumari Raj Yoga Centre
- New Rohtak Rd.
- Sidipura
- Idgah Chk.
- SS Sch.
- SS Sch.
- Dharma Pratap Rd.
- Ganeshwar Dham Mg.
- Tytler HS. Sch.
- Rani Jhansi Rd.
- Shahi Idgah
- Idgah Rd.
- KAROL BAGH
- Ajmal Khan Park
- Dr. Narain Chand Joshi
- East Park Rd.
- Khaibar Mg.
- Dargah Mamoo Bhanja
- Shahi Idgah Clny.
- Sant Sugan Chand Mg.
- Gurudwara Rd.
- Jhandewalan Rd.
- Nabi Karim
- Gautam
- Deshbandhu Gupta Rd.
- Pal Mohan Plaza
- Motia Khan Dump Scheme
- Dimple
- Girl's SS Sch.
- Joshi Rd.
- Punjabi Academy
- Bagichi Allauddin
- Dr. Ram Manohar Lohia Mg.

Grid 3

- Sobti
- Beadonpura
- Rul Aziz Rd.
- JHANDEWALAN
- Library
- Sadar Thana Rd.
- Rajasthan
- Sri Kishan Doss Mg.
- Pyare Lal Mg.
- Faiz Chk.
- Mata Mandir
- ESS Aar Motors
- Motaikhan
- Arya Samaj Rd.
- Hardhyan Singh Mg.
- Abdul Rahman Mg.
- Nai Walan
- Lakshmi Mahavidyalaya
- Indian Inst. of Packaging
- Sant Nirankari SS Sch.
- Multani Dhanda
- First
- SS Sch.
- Ashoka Pahari
- MM Rd.
- Sat Biramani Rd.
- SB Arya Sch.
- Girl's SS Sch.
- Bharti Mahila Col.
- Swami Ramtirth Nagar
- Deen Dayal Research Inst.
- Aram Bagh Rd.
- Sadhu Vasvani Mg.
- Dayal Chk.
- Ridge Rd.
- SS Sch.
- Jhandewalan Extn.
- Vallabhacharya Mg.
- Ramjas HS. Sch.
- Pahar Ganj
- DAV Col.
- Link Rd.
- Jagjivan Ram Vidya Bvn.
- Bhuli Bhatiyari
- Meghdoot Bhawan
- Aram Bagh
- Govt Girl's SS Sch.
- Darbari Lal Mg.
- Chitragupta Rd.
- Raigarh Mg.
- Sant Asa Ram Bapu Ashram
- Ekant
- Chuna Mandi
- Devi's Col.

C | **D**

23

Old Delhi

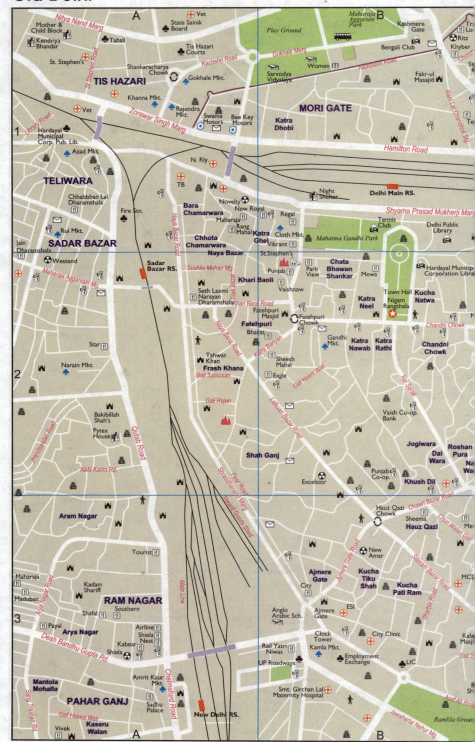

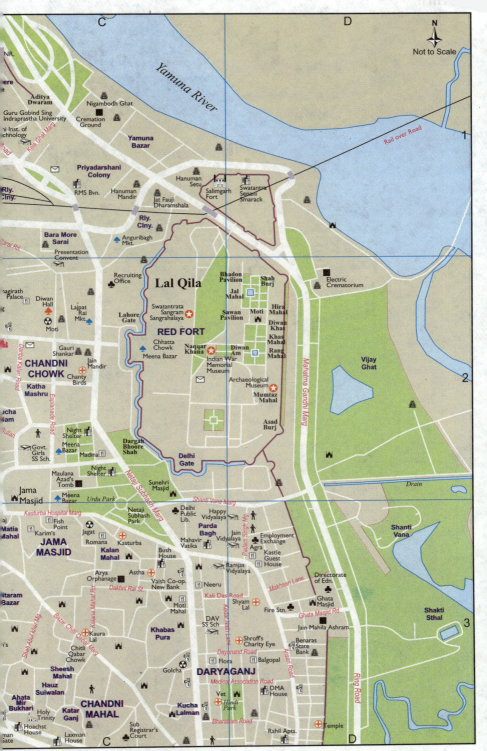

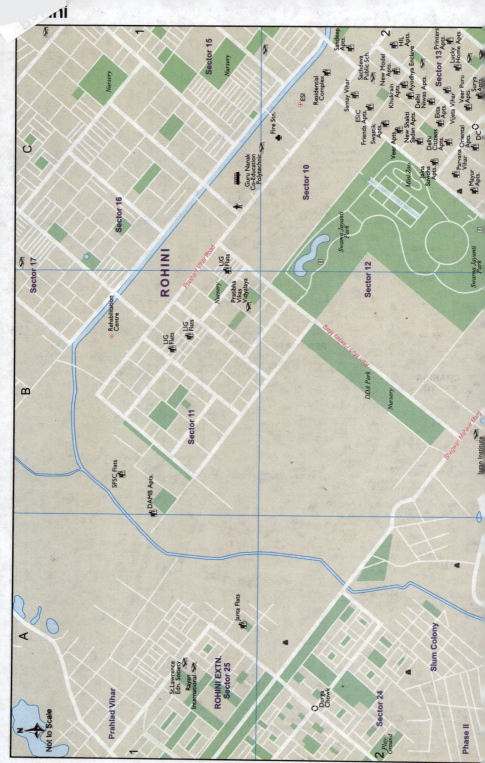

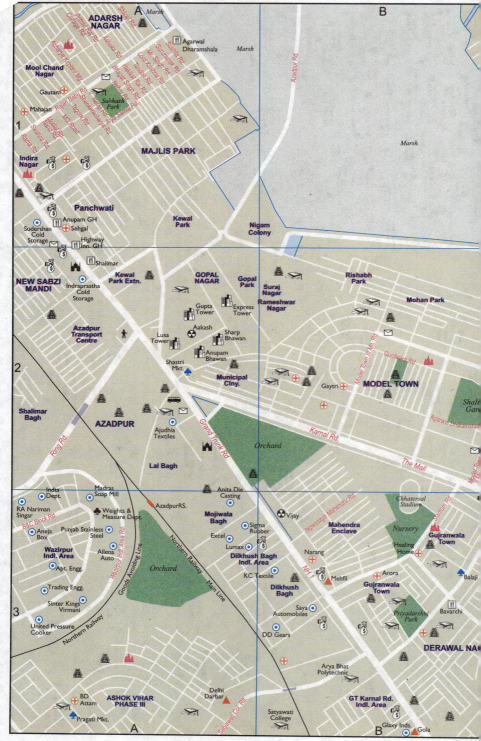

Mustafabad, Shahdara

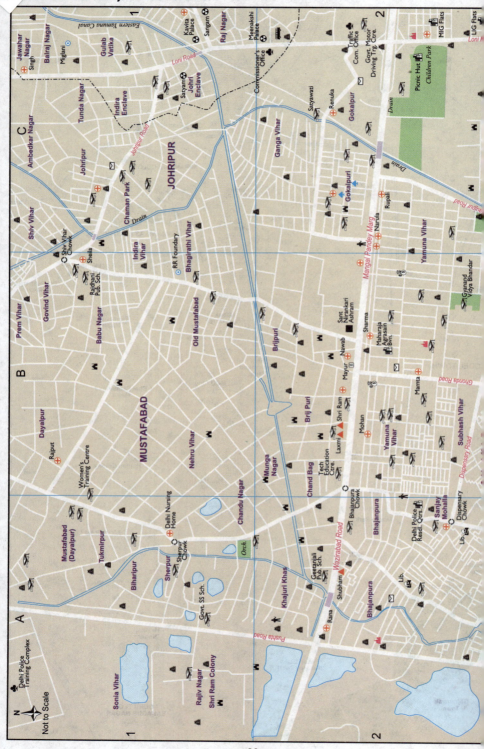

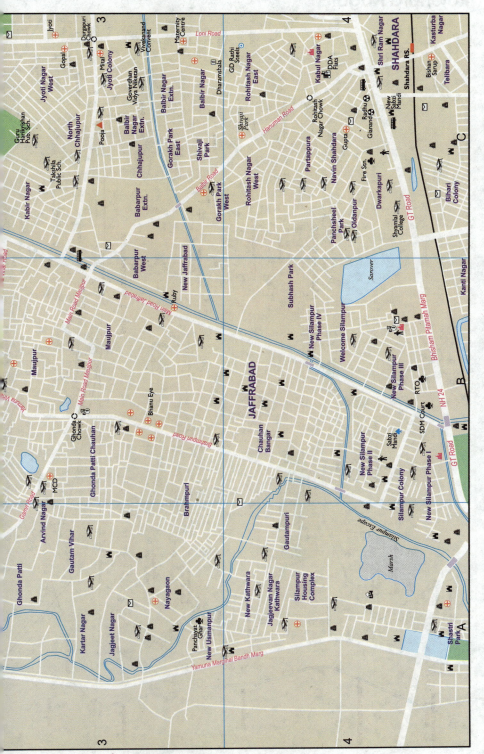

Rajendra Nagar

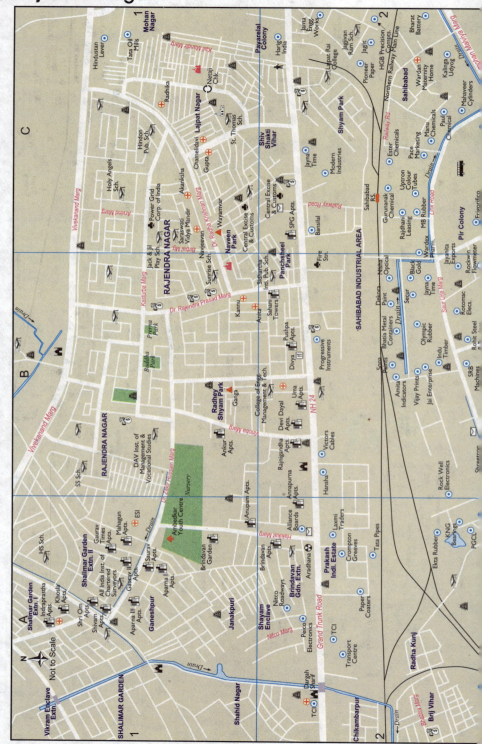

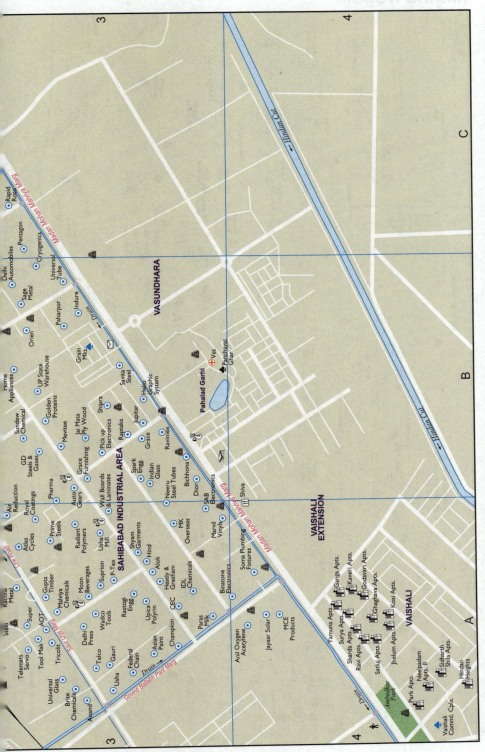

Krishna Nagar

Janakpuri

Qutb Institutional Area

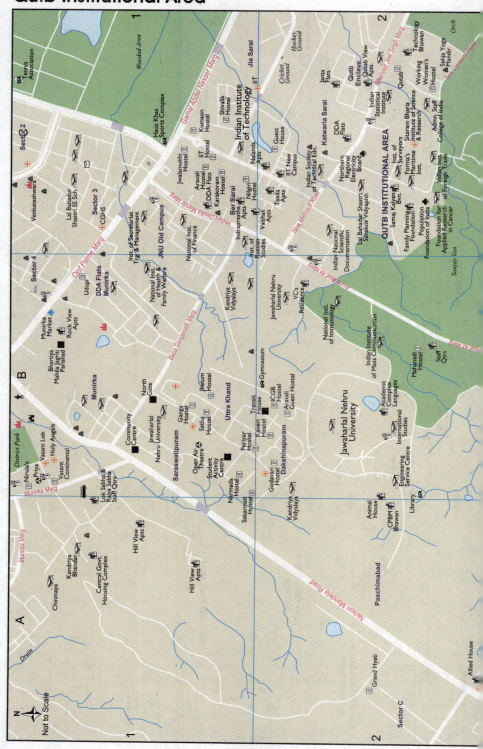

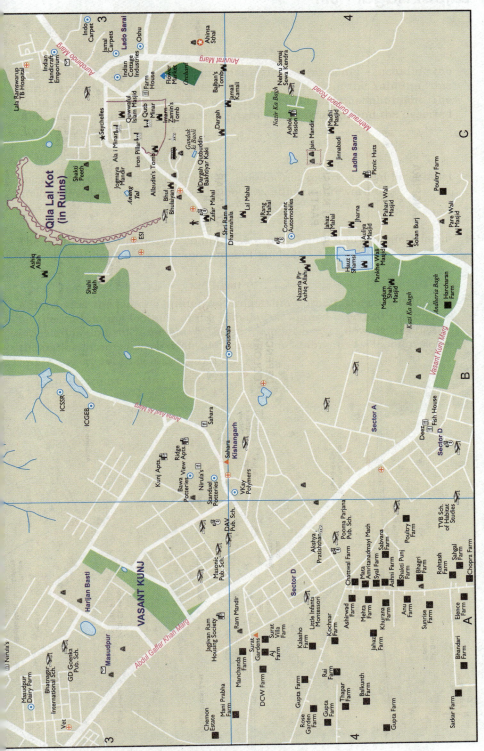

Lajpat Nagar - Siri

Tughlakabad

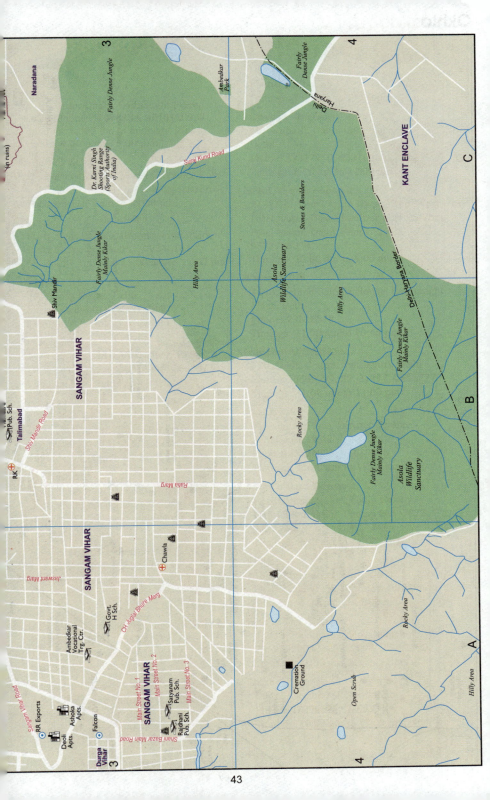

Okhla

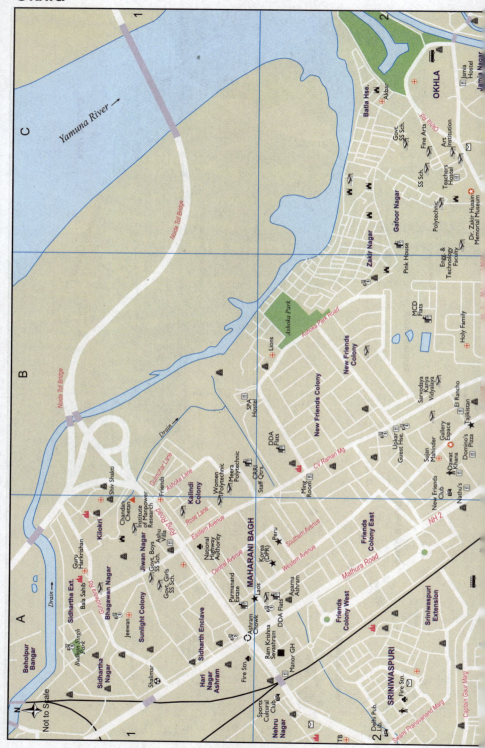

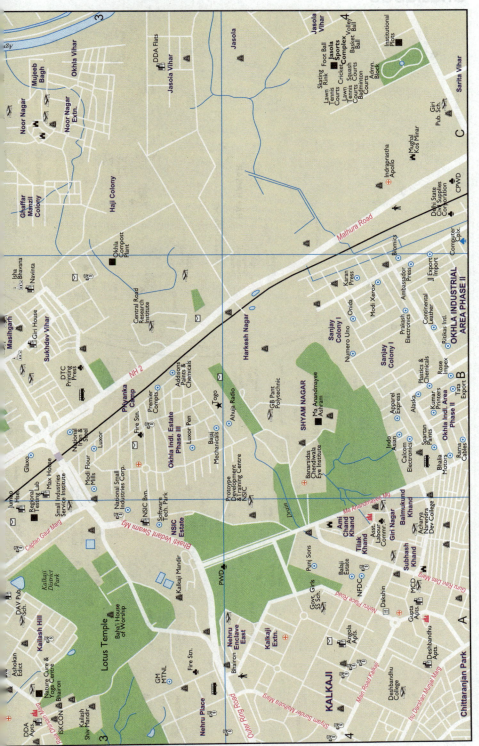

Ghaziabad

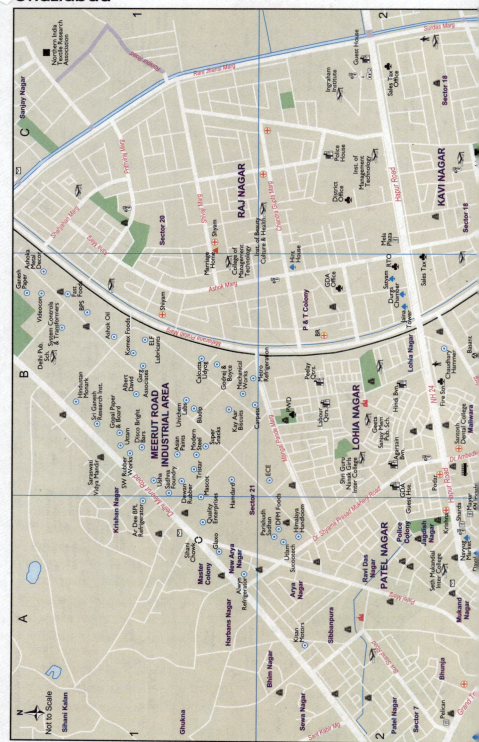

Faridabad

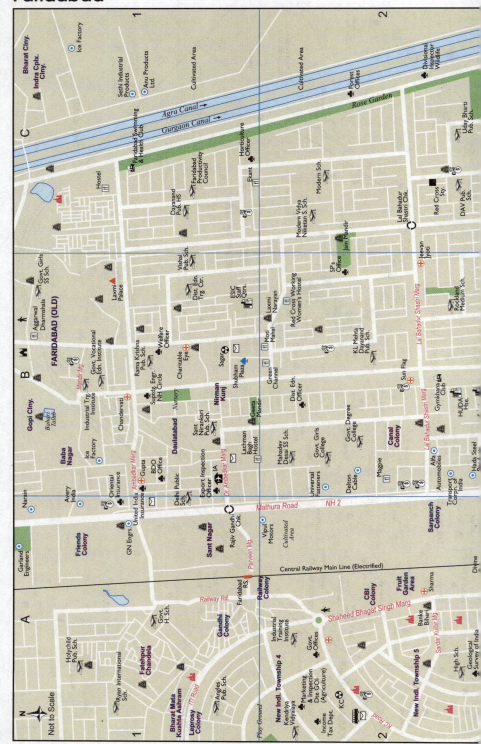

Gurgaon

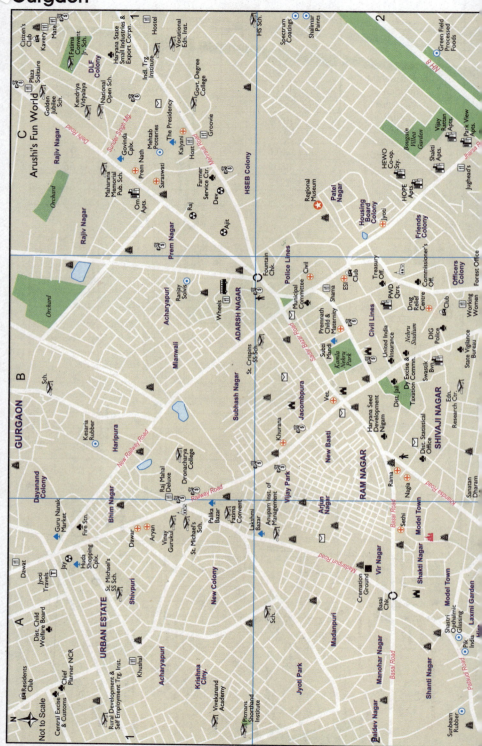

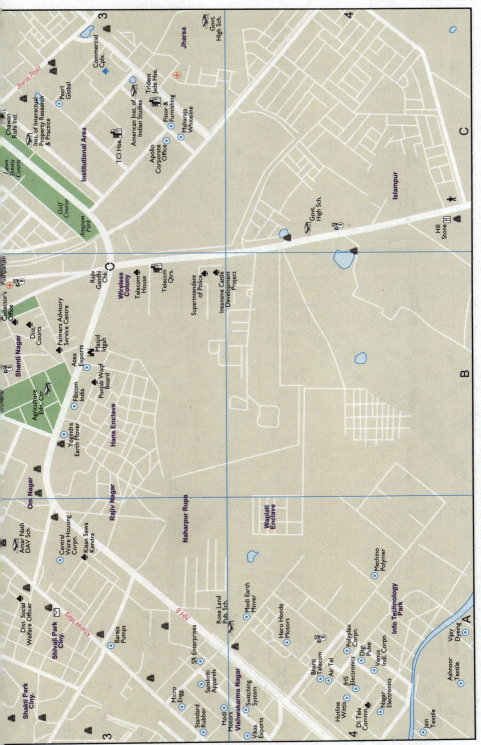

Noida

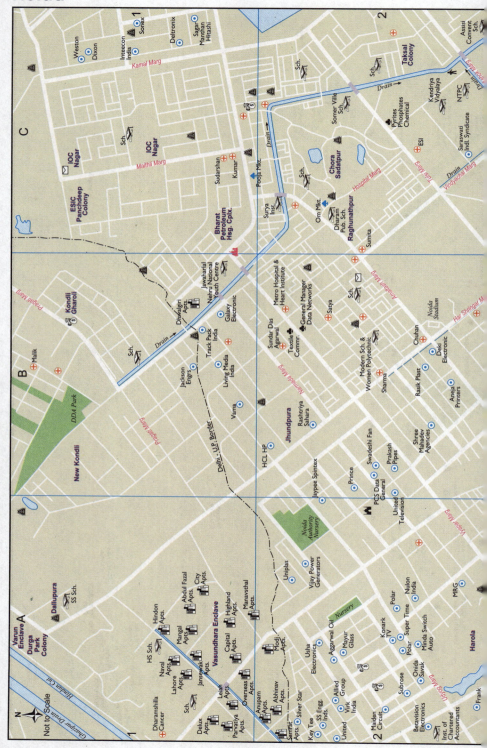

AREA NAMES					
Acharyapuri	50 A1 50 B1	Balbir Nagar	31 C3	Chankaya Place Part I	36 A2
Adarsh Nagar	28 A1	Baldev Nagar	50 A2	Chata Bhawan Shankar	24 B2
Adarsh Nagar	50 B1	Baldev Park	34 AB2	Chauhan Bangar	31 B4
Ahata Mir Bukhari	25 C3	Balmiki Basti	20 C1	Chhajupur	31 C3
Ajay Enclave	36 C1	Balmiki Clny.	22 B3	Chhota Chamarwara	24 A1
Ajmere Gate	24 B3	Balmukund Khand	45 AB4	Chikambarpur	32 A2
Ajronda	49 B3 49 A3	Balraj Nagar	30 C1	Chirag Enclave	41 C4
Alaknanda	42 B1	Bank Enclave	35 A3	Chiragh Delhi	41 B4
Aliganj	40 A1	Bapa Nagar	21 B3	Chitra Vihar	34 AB2
Amar Colony	40 C2	Bapu Dham	18 A2	Chittaranjan Park	41 C4 45 A4
Ambedkar Nagar	30 C1	Bara Chamarwara	24 A1	Chora Sadatpur	52 C2
Ambedkar Camp	35 C4	Bara Hindu Rao	23 D1	Chota Kaila	47 A3
Ami Chand Khand	45 A4	Bara More Sarai	25 C1	Chowk Nai Basti	23 D1-2
Amrit Nagar	40 A1	Barracks	20 B2	Chuna Mandi	23 D3
Amritpuri (Garhi)	41 C3	Basant Ln. Rly. Clny.	20 A1	Civil Aviation Colony	40 A1
Anand Kunj	36 A1	Batla Hse.	44 C2	Civil Lines	50 B2
Anand Lok	41 A3	Beadonpura	23 C3	Connaught Place	20 A1
Anand Parbat	22 A1	Beholpur Bangar	44 A1	Dabri Extn. East	37 B3
Anand Vihar	34 C2 36 C1	Ber Sarai	38 C1	Dabri Extn.	37 B3
Anarkali Clny. North	34 B2	Bhagawan Nagar	44 A1	Dabri	37 B3
Anarkali Clny. South	34 AB2	Bhagirathi Vihar	30 BC1	Dada Bari	39 C4
Andrews Ganj Extension	40 B2	Bhai Parmanand Nagar	29 D2	Dai Wara	24 B2
Andrews Ganj	40 B2	Bhajanpura	30 A2	Dakshinapuram	38 A2
Anna Nagar	20 C2	Bharat Clny.	48 C1	Dakshinpuri Extn.	42 A1
Anup Nagar	36 A2	Bharat Mata Kushta Ashram	48 A1	Dakshinpuri	42 A1
Ar Colony	19 A4	Bharat Petroleum Hsg. Cplx.	52 C1	Dallupura	52 A1
Aram Bagh	23 D3	Bharti Clny.	35 B3	Daryaganj	25 CD3
Aram Ganj	23 D1	Bharti Nagar	21 B4	Dasna Gate	47 A3
Aram Nagar	24 A3	Bhel Colony	52 A3	Dasrathpuri	37 B3
Arjun Nagar	34 B1 40 B1 47 B3 50 A2	Bhikaji Cama Place	19 B4	Daulatabad	48 B1
Arjun Ngr. East	34 B1	Bhim Nagar	46 A2 50 A1	Daulatpura	47 B4
Arun Vihar	52 BC4	Bhola Nagar	40 A1	Dayalpur	30 B1
Arvind Nagar	31 A3	Bhoomi Heen Camp	42 BC1	Dayanand Colony	40 C2 50 B1
Arya Nagar	24 A3 34 C2 46 A2 47 B4	Bhuli Bhatiyari	23 C3	Dayanand Nagar	47 B3
Asaltpur Khadar	36 A2	Bhunja	46 A2	Dayanand Vihar	34 C2
Asha Park	36 C1	Bhur Bharat Nagar	47 A4	Dda Flats Masjid Moth Ph. I	41 B4
Ashok Nagar	36 C1 47 C3	Bihari Colony	31 C4	Dda Flats Munirka	38 BC1
Ashok Vihar Phase III	28 A3	Bihari Nagar	47 A3	Deepali	27 B4
Ashoka Niketan	34 C1	Biharipur	30 A1	Defence Colony	40 B1
Ashoka Pahari	23 C3	Bindapur	37 B3	Defence Enclave	35 B3
Asiad Centre	41 A3	Bk Dutt Colony	40 A1	Delhi Gate	25 C2
Asian Games Village Complex	41 A3	Brahampuri	37 C3 31 AB3	Deoli Extension	42 A2
Atta	52 A4	Brij Puri	30 B2	Deoli Gaon Nai Basti	43 A3
Ayurvigyan Nagar	41 A3	Brij Vihar	32 A2	Derawal Nagar	28 B3 29 C3
Azad Colony	48 B2	Brijpuri	30 B2 34 A2	Dev Nagar	22 B2
Azad Market	23 D1	Brindavan Gdn. Extn.	32 A2	Dhaka Clny.	29 D2
Azad Nagar East	34 A1	Budh Vihar	27 A3	Dharam Pura	24 B2
Azad Nagar West	34 A1	Budhela	36 A1	Dhirpur (Dhaka)	29 D1
Azad Nagar	23 C1	Canal Colony	48 B2	Dilkhush Bagh Indl. Area	28 B3
Azadpur Transport Centre	28 A2	Cbi Colony	48 A2	Dilkhush Bagh	28 B3
Azadpur	28 A2	Chaman Park	30 C1	Diplomatic Enclave	18 B1
Baba Nagar	48 B1	Chanakyapuri	18 B2 19 B3	Diz Area	20 A1
Babarpur Extn.	31 C3	Chand Bag	30 B2	Dlf Colony	50 C1
Babarpur West	31 B3	Chandar Nagar	36 A1-2	Dori Walan	23 C2
Babu Nagar	30 B1	Chander Vihar	35 B3	Dr. Ambedkar Nagar	42 A1
Bagh Bhathyari	47 B3	Chandni Chowk	24 B2 25 C2	Dr. Mukherjee Nagar	29 D2
Bagichi Allauddin	23 D3	Chandni Mahal	25 C3	Durga Park Colony	52 A1
Bahubali Enclave	34 C1	Chandra Nagar	34 A2	Durga Vihar	43 A3
Bajriyan	47 A3	Chandra Shekhar Azad Clny.	23 C1	Dwarka	37 A4
Balbir Nagar Extn.	31 C3	Chandrapuri	47 A3	Dwarkapuri	31 C4
		Chandu Nagar	30 AB1	East Block	19 AB4

East End Enclave	34 A2	Gujranwala Town	28 B3 29 C3	Janakpuri District Centre	36 A1
East Krishna Nagar	34 B1	Gulab Vatika	30 C1	Janakpuri	32 A1 36 A2 36 B1
East Of Kailash	41 C3 45 A3	Gurgaon	50 B1		36 B2 36 BC1 36 C2 37 B3 37 C3
East Patel Nagar	22 A3	Guru Nanak Ngr.	35 A3	Jangpura	40 C1
Ekta Vihar	19 A4	Guru Ram Das Nagar	35 A3	Jasola Vihar	45 C3 45 C4
Electronic Nagar	52 A3	Guru Teg Bahadur Nagar	29 D3	Jasola	45 C4
Esic Panchdeep Colony	52 C1	Gyan Kunj	35 A3	Jassipura	47 A3
Fajalpur	35 B4	Haji Colony	45 C3	Jatwara	47 AB3
Faridabad (Old)	48 B1	Hakikat Nagar	29 D3	Jawahar Nagar	30 C1
Fateh Nagar	36 B1 36 C1	Hamdard Nagar	42 B2	Jeevan Park	36 A2
Fatehpur Chandela	48 A1	Hans Enclave	51 B3	Jhandapur	33 B3
Fatehpuri	24 AB2	Harbans Nagar	46 A1	Jhandewalan Extn.	23 D3
Frash Khana	24 A2	Hardware Clny.	49 A4	Jhandewalan	23 D3
Friends Colony East	44 A2	Hargobind Enclave	34 Bc2	Jharsa	51 C3
Friends Colony West	44 A2	Hari Nagar Ashram	44 A1	Jhundpura	52 B2
Friends Colony	48 A1 48 C2 50 C2	Hari Nagar	36 C1 36c2	Jia Sarai	38 C1
Fruit Garden Area	48 A2	Harijan Basti	19 A4 30 C2	Jitar Nagar	34 B2
Fruit Garden	49 A3		39 A3 52 B4 37 C4	Jiwan Nagar	44 A1
Fyaz Ganj	23 D1	Harijan Colony	29 D2	JNU Old Campus	38 C1
Gafoor Nagar	44 C2	Haripura	50 B1	Jogiwara	24 B2
Gagan Vihar	34 B2	Harkesh Nagar	45 B4	Johri Enclave	30 C1
Galek Chand	47 B3	Harola	52 A2	Johripur	30 C1
Ganda Nala	47 A3	Haryana Estate	20 B1	Joshi Clny.	35 C3
Gandhi Colony	48 A1	Hasanpur (Nangla)	35 C3	Jyoti Colony	31 C3
Gandhi Nagar	47 B4 51 A3	Hathi Khana	23 D1	Jyoti Nagar West	31 C3
Ganesh Nagar I South	35 A4	Hauz Qazi	24 B3	Jyoti Park	50 A2
Ganesh Nagar II	35 A4	Hauz Suiwalan	25 C3	Kabir Nagar	31 C3
Ganesh Nagar	35 A4 36 B1	Hemkunt Colony	41 C3	Kabul Nagar	31 C3
Ganeshpur	32 A1	Hira Nagar	50 A2	Kaila Bhatta	47 A3
Ganga Vihar	30 C2	Housing Board Colony	50 C2	Kailash Hill	45 A3
Gaupuri	47 A3	Hseb Colony	50 C1	Kailash Nagar	47 A3
Gaushala	47 A3	Hudco Place	40 AB2	Kailashpuri East.	37 C4
Gautam Nagar	40 A2	Hydel Colony	46 B2	Kailashpuri Main.	37 C4
Gautam Puri	20 C1	Ina Clny.	19 C4	Kailashpuri West	37 B4
Gautam Vihar	31 A3	Indira Enclave	30 C1	Kaka Nagar	21 B3
Gautampuri	31 A4	Indira Nagar	28 A1	Kalan Mahal	25 C3
Geeta Colony	34 A2	Indira Vihar	30 BC1	Kalindi Colony	44 AB1
Geetanjali Park	37 C3	Indira Vikas Colony	29 D1	Kalka Garhi	47 B3
Ghaffar Manzil Colony	45 C3	Indra Cplx. Clny.	48 C1	Kalkaji Dda Flats	42 B1
Ghonda Patti Chauhan	31 B3	Indra Park Extn.	37 C4	Kalkaji Extn.	42 C1 45 A4
Ghonda Patti	31 A3	Indra Park.	37 C4	Kallupura	47 B3
Ghondli	34 A1	Indraprastha Extn.	35 B4 35 C3	Kalyanvas	35 C4
Ghukna	46 A1	Info Technology Park	51 A4	Kamal Park.	37 C4
Giri Nagar	45 A4	Institutional Area	51 C3	Kamala Nagar	47 C4
Gokalpur	30 C2	IOC Nagar	52 C1	Kangra Niketan	36 A1
Gopal Nagar	28 A2 36 C1	IP Estate	20 C2	Kant Enclave	43 C4
Gopal Park	28 A2 34 A2	Ishwar Nagar	45 B3 47 A3	Kanti Nagar	31 B4
Gopal Vihar	27 A3	Islampur	51 C4	Kardam Puri	30 C2
Gopi Clny.	48 B1	Jacombpura	50 B2	Karkar Duma	34 C2
Gorakh Park East	31 C3	Jaffrabad	31 B4	Karkar Mandan	33 A3
Gorakh Park West	31 C3	Jagat Ram Park	35 A3	Karol Bagh West Extn. Area	37 C4
Govind Park	34 B2	Jagatpuri	34 B2	Karol Bagh	22 B3 23 C2
Govind Vihar	30 B1	Jagdamba Vihar	37 Bc4	Kartar Nagar	31 A3
Greater Kailash Enclave I	41 C4	Jagdish Nagar	46 A2	Kaseru Walan	24 A3
Greater Kailash Enclave II	41 B4	Jagjeet Nagar	31 A3	Kashmere Gate	25 C1
Greater Kailash I	41 B3	Jagjeevan Nagar	31 A4	Kasturba Nagar (Sewa Nagar)	40 B1
Greater Kailash II	41 C4	Jagriti Enclave	34 C2	Kasturba Nagar	31 C4
Greater Kailash III (Masjid Moth)	41 B4	Jaiprakash Nagar	47 C4	Kasturba Niketan	40 C2
Gt Karnal Rd. Indl. Area	28 B3	Jal Vayu Vihar	52 B2 52 B3	Katar Ganj	25 C3
Gujarat Vihar	34 B2	Jama Masjid	25 C3	Katha Mashru	25 C2
Gujranwala Town	28 B3	Jamia Nagar	44 C2 45 C3	Kathwara	31 A4

Location	Ref	Location	Ref	Location	Ref
Katra Dhobi	24 B1	Maharishi Enclave.	37 C4	Municipal Clny.	28 A2
Katra Ghel	24 AB1	Mahavir Colony	37 B3	Munirka	38 B1
Katra Nawab	24 B2	Mahavir Enclave I	37 A4	Munshiram Dairy Clny.	29 D2
Katra Neel	24 B2	Mahavir Enclave II	37 A4	Mustafabad (Dayalpur)	30 A1
Katra Rathi	24 B2	Mahavir Enclave III	37 B3	Mustafabad	30 B1
Katwaria Sarai	38 C2	Mahavir Nagar New	36 Ab1	Nabi Karim	23 D2
Kavi Nagar Industrial Area	47 C3	Mahavir Nagar Old	36 B1	Naharpur Rupa	51 A3
Kavi Nagar	46 C2 47 C3	Mahendra Enclave	28 B3	Naharpur	27 B4
Kewal Park Extn.	28 A2	Mahindra Park	36 A2	Nai Basti	47 A3
Kewal Park	28 A1	Majlis Park	28 A1	Nai Wala	24 B2
Khabas Pura	25 C3	Malikpur	29 C2	Nai Walan	23 C3
Khajuri Khas	30 A2	Maliwara	46 B2	Nanak Pura	36 C1
Khanpur	42 A2	Manak Vihar Extn.	36 C1	Nanak Ram Clny.	29 D2
Khari Baoli	24 Ab2	Manak Vihar	36 C1	Nangal Raya	37 C3
Khichripur	35 C4	Mandakini Enclave	42 B1	Nangli Jalib	36 B1
Khush Dil	24 B2	Mandaoli	35 B4	Naradana	43 C3
Kidwai Nagar East	40 A2	Mangalam Place	27 B4	Narang Clny.	36 A1
Kidwai Nagar West	19 C4	Manglapuri II	37 B4	Narayan Nagar	35 A3
Kilokri	44 A1	Mangolpur Kalan	27 Ab4	Narsirpur	37 B4 47 C3
Kiran Vihar	34 BC1-2	Mangolpur Khurd	27 A4	Nasrat Pura	47 A3
Kishan Ganj	23 C1	Mangolpuri	27 A4	National Park	40 B2
Kishangarh	39 B4	Manohar Nagar	50 A2	Nauroji Nagar	19 B4
Kondli Gharoli	52 B1	Mantola Mohalla	24 A3	Naveen Park	32 C1
Kotgoan	47 B4	Masihgarh	45 B3	Navin Shahdara	31 C4
Kotla Mubarakpur	40 A1	Masjid Moth	40 A2 41 B4	Nawab Ganj	23 D1
Krishan Kunj	35 A3	Master Colony	46 A1	Naya Bazar	24 A1-2
Krishan Nagar	46 A1	Masudpur	39 A3	Naya Ganj	47 B3
Krishna Clny.	50 A1	Mata Colony	47 A4	Naya Mohalla	23 D1
Krishna Nagar Extn.	34 A2	Mata Rameshwari Nehru Clny.	22 B3	Nayagaon	31 A3
Krishna Nagar	22 B2 34 A1 49 A3	Mata Sundari Railway Clny.	20 B1	Nazar Ali	47 A3
Krishna Park	36 A1	Matia Mahal	25 C3	Neeti Bagh	41 A3
Kucha Alam	25 C2	Maujpur	31 B3	Nehru Enclave East	45 A4
Kucha Lalman	25 C3	Mausam Vihar	34 B2	Nehru Nagar II	47 B3
Kucha Natwa	24 B2	Mawai	47 A4	Nehru Nagar III	47 BC4
Kucha Pati Ram	24 B3	Maya Enclave	36 C2	Nehru Nagar	40 C2 44 A2
Kucha Tiku Shah	24 B3	Mayur Vihar Phase II	35 B4	Nehru Place	41 C3 45 A3
Kundan Nagar	34 A2	Mcd Clny.	29 C3 29 D2	Nehru Vihar	30 B1
Ladha Sarai	39 C4	Meena Bagh	21 A3	Netaji Nagar	19 B4
Lado Sarai	39 C3	Meerut Road Industrial Area	46 B1	New Arya Nagar	46 A1
Lajpat Nagar Part I	40 C1	Mianwali	50 B1	New Basti	50 B4
Lajpat Nagar Part II	40 C2	Mirzapur	37 B3 47 A4	New Colony	50 A1
Lajpat Nagar Part III	40 B2	Model Basti	23 C2	New Friends Colony	44 B2
Lajpat Nagar Part IV	40 C2	Model Town	28 B2 29 C2 47 B4 50 A2	New Govindpura	34 A2
Lajpat Nagar	32 C1	Mohammadpur	19 B4	New Indl. Township 1	49 A4
Lajwanti Garden	37 C3	Mohan Nagar	32 C1 37 C3	New Indl. Township 4	48 A2
Lakshmi Ngr.	35 A3 35 A3 19 C3	Mohan Park	28 B2 35 A3	New Indl. Township 5	48 A2 49 A3
Lal Bagh	28 A2	Moheman Sarai	47 B4	New Indl. Township	49 A3
Lalita Park	35 A3	Mojiwala Bagh	28 A3	New Jaffrabad	31 A4
Laxmi Garden	50 A2	Mool Chand Nagar	28 A1	New Kathwara	31 A4
Lekha Vihar	19 B4	Mori Gate	24 B1	New Kondli	52 B1
Leprosy Colony	48 A1	Motaikhan	23 D3	New Layalpur Clny.	34 Ab2
Lodi Estate	20 AB4	Moti Bagh Indl. Area	22 A1	New Rajdhani Enclave	34 B2
Loha Mandi	47 C4	Moti Bagh North	19 A3	New Sabzi Mandi	28 A2
Lohia Nagar	46 B2	Moti Bagh South	19 A3	New Silampur Phase I	31 Ab4
Madangir Camp	42 A2	Moti Bagh	22 B1	New Silampur Phase II	31 B4
Madangir	42 A1	Motia Bagh Rly. Clny.	23 D1	New Silampur Phase III	31 B4
Madanpuri	37 BC3 50 A2	Motia Khan Dump Scheme	23 D2	New Silampur Phase IV	31 B4
Madhu Vihar	35 C3	Mujeeb Bagh	45 C3	New Usmanpur	31 A3
Madhuban Enclave	35 B3	Mukand Nagar	46 A2	Nigam Colony	28 AB1
Madhupura	47 A4	Multani Dhanda	23 D3	Nirankari Colony	29 D1
Maharani Bagh	44 A1	Munga Nagar	30 B2	Nirman Kunj	48 B1

Location	Ref	Location	Ref	Location	Ref
Nirman Vihar	35 B3	Prem Nagar	36 BC1 40 A1	Safdarjang Aerodrome	19 C3
Nithari	52 C3	Prem Nagar	47 A3 50 C1	Safdarjang Enclave	19 B4
Nizamuddin West	21 C4	Prem Vihar	30 B1	Sagarpur East.	37 C4
Noor Nagar Extn.	45 C3	President's Estate	18 B1	Sagarpur Main	37 C3
Noor Nagar	45 C3	Priya Enclave	34 B2	Sagarpur West	37 C3
North Chhajupur	31 C3	Priyadarshani Colony	25 C1	Sahibabad	32 C2
Northern Railway Colony	18 A2	Priyadarshini Vihar	34 A2	Sahibabad Industrial Area	32 B2 33 A3
NSIC Estate	45 A3	Priyanka Camp	45 B3	Saini Enclave	34 C2
Officers Colony	50 B2	Punjabi Basti	22 A2	Sangam Vihar	42 AB2 43 A3 43 B3
Okhla Indl. Area Ph I	42 C1	Pushpanjali Enclave	27 B4	Sanjay Amar Clny.	20 C2
Okhla Indl. Area Phase II	45 B4	Pushpanjali	34 C1	Sanjay Colony I	45 B4
Okhla Indl. Estate Phase III	45 B3	Qila Lal Kot (In Ruins)	39 C3	Sanjay Mohalla	30 A2
Okhla Industrial Area Phase II	45 B4	Qutb Enclave	38 C2	Sanjay Nagar	46 C1
Okhla Vihar	45 C3	Qutb Institutional Area	38 C2	Sant Nagar	41 C3 48 A1
Okhla	44 C2	Rabindra Nagar	21 A4	Sanwal Nagar	41 B3
Old Mustafabad	30 B1	Radha Kunj	32 A2	Sarai Nagar	47 A3
Oldanpur	31 C4	Radhey Shyam Park	32 B1 34 AB2	Sarai Rohilla	22 B1
Om Nagar	51 B3	Radheypuri	34 B1	Saraswati Vihar	27 C4
Outram Lines	29 D3	Raghu Nagar	37 B3	Saraswatipuram	38 B1
P & T Colony	46 B2 36 A1	Raghunathpur	52 C2	Sarita Vihar	45 C4
Padam Nagar	22 B1	Railway Clny.	20 C2 22 A1 22 B1 23 D1 47 A3 48 A2	Sarojini Nagar	19 B4
Pahalad Garhi	33 B3			Sarojini Park	34 A2
Pahar Ganj	23 D3 24 A3	Railway Officers Clny.	23 C1	Sarojini Vihar	19 C4
Pahari Dhiraj	23 D2	Railway Qtrs.	23 C1	Sarpanch Colony	48 A2
Palika Niketan	19 A4	Railway Station Colony	47 B4	Sat Nagar	22 B3
Palika Niwas	40 A1	Raj Nagar	19 C4 30 C1 46 C1	Savitri Nagar	41 A4
Palika Vihar	18 B1	Rajeev Park.	37 C4	Sector 1	27 A4 47 A3
Pamposh Enclave	41 C4	Rajendra Nagar	22 B3 32 B1 32 BC1	Sector 10	26 C2
Panchsheel Enclave	41 B4	Rajendra Place	22 A3	Sector 11	26 B1
Panchsheel Park	31 C4	Rajgarh Colony	34 A1	Sector 12	26 B2
Panchsheel Park	32 B2	Rajiv Nagar	30 A1 50 C1 51 A3	Sector 13	26 C2
Panchshila Park North	41 A4	Ram Bagh	23 D1	Sector 14 Extn.	27 C3
Panchshila Park South	41 A4	Ram Nagar	24 A3 34 A1 47 B3 49 A4 50 B2	Sector 14	27 C3
Panchwati	28 A1			Sector 15	26 C1
Pandara Park	21 B3	Ram Vihar	34 C1 52 B3	Sector 16	26 C1
Pandav Nagar	35 A4	Ramakrishnapuram	19 A4	Sector 17	26 Bc1 47 C4
Pandit Park	34 A1	Ramesh Park	35 A3	Sector 18	46 C2
Parda Bagh	25 C3	Rameshwar Nagar	28 B2	Sector 2	27 AB4 38 C1 47 B3
Partappura	31 C4	Rani Garden	34 A2	Sector 20	46 C1
Paschimabad	38 A2	Ravi Das Nagar	46 A2	Sector 21	46 Ab1
Pataudi House	20 A2	Razapur	27 C3	Sector 24	26 A2
Patel Dham	18 A2	Red Fort	25 C2	Sector 25	26 A1
Patel Nagar	46 A2 50 C2	Rehgarpura	22 B3	Sector 3	27 B4 38 C1 47 B3 47 BC4
Patparganj Industrial Area	35 C3	Rishab Vihar	34 C1	Sector 4	27 A3 38 B1 47 C4
Payarelal Colony	32 Bc2	Rishabh Park	28 B2	Sector 5	27 B3 47 B4
Phase I	27 A3	Rithala	26 A2	Sector 6	27 B3 47 A3
Phase II	26 A2	Rly. Clny.	25 C1 40 B1	Sector 7	27 BC3 46 A2
Pillanji	19 C3	Rohini Avantika	27 A4	Sector 8	27 C4
Pir Colony	32 C2	Rohini Extn.	26 A1	Sector 9	27 C3 47 A4
Pk Rd. Rly. Clny.	20 A1	Rohini Institutional Area	27 B4	Sector A	39 B4
Police Colony	19 A4 40 A2 46 A2	Rohini	26 BC1 27 BC3	Sector B	39 A3
Police Lines (Kingsway Camp)	29 C3 50 B2	Rohitash Nagar East	31 C4	Sector C	38 A2
		Rohitash Nagar West	31 C4	Sector D	39 A4 39 B4
Police Residential Clny.	29 C3	Roshan Pura	24 B2	Sector I	41 B3
Poshangipur	36 B2	Rouse Avenue	20 B1	Sector II	41 Ab3
Pragati Maidan	21 C3	Sabzi Mandi	23 D1	Sector III	41 Ab3
Prahlad Vihar	26 A1	Sadar Bazar	23 D2 24 A1	Sewa Nagar	46 A2
Prakash Indl. Estate	32 A2	Sadh Nagar I	37 B4	Shah Ganj	24 Ab2
Prasad Nagar	22 A3	Sadh Nagar II	37 B4	Shahdara	31 C4
Pratap Nagar	36 C2	Sadh Nagar Part II	37 B4	Shaheed Camp	42 A2
Preet Vihar	35 B3	Sadiq Nagar	41 B3	Shahi Idgah Clny.	23 D2

Name	Ref	Name	Ref	Name	Ref
Shahid Nagar	32 A1	Subhash Khand	45 A4	Vikram Enclave Extn.	32 A1
Shahpur Jat	41 A4	Subhash Mohalla	30 B2	Vikram Nagar	20 C1
Shakarpur Extn.	35 A3	Subhash Park	31 B4	Vikram Vihar	40 B2
Shakarpur Khas	35 A3	Subhash Vihar	30 B2	Vinoba Prui	40 C2
Shakarpur	35 A4	Sujan Singh Park North	21 B3	Vinod Ngr. East	35 C4
Shakti Nagar	50 A2	Sujan Singh Park	21 B4	Vinod Ngr. West	35 B4
Shakti Park Clny.	51 A3	Sukh Vihar	34 B2	Vir Nagar	50 A2
Shakti Sthal	25 D3	Sukhdev Vihar	45 B3	Virendra Nagar	36c2
Shalimar Bagh	28 A2	Sundar Nagar	21 C4	Vishwakarma Nagar	51 A4
Shalimar Garden Extn. I	32 A1	Sundarpuri	47 A4	Vishwakarma Park	35 A3
Shalimar Garden Extn. II	32 A1	Sunder Park	34 AB1	Vishwas Nagar Extension	34 B1
Shalimar Garden	32 A1	Sunlight Colony	44 A1	Vishwas Nagar	34 B1
Shankar Garden	36 A1	Suraj Nagar	28 B2	Vishwas Ngr. Extn.	34 B1
Shankar Nagar Extn.	34 A1	Surajmal Vihar	34 C1	Vivekanand Nagar	47 A4
Shankar Nagar West	34 A1	Surya Niketan	34 C1	Vivekanand Puri	22 B1
Shankar Nagar	34 A1	Swami Ramtirth Nagar	23 D3	Wapiati Enclave	51 A4
Shanti Mohalla	34 A1	Swasthya Vihar	34 B2	Wazir Nagar	40 AB2
Shanti Nagar	50 A2 51 B3	Syndicate Enclave	37 B3	Wazirpur Indl. Area	28 A3
Shanti Vana	25 D3	Tagore Park Extn.	29 C3	Welcome Silampur	31 B4
Sharad Vihar	34 C2	Tagore Park	29 C2	West Block	19 A4
Shastri Nagar	34 A2	Taksal Colony	52 C2	West Chandra Nagar	34 A2
Shastri Park	31 A4 34 A1	Talimabad	43 B3	Wireless Colony	51 B3
Shayam Enclave	32 A2	Tarun Enclave	27 B4	Yamuna Bazar	25 C1
Sheesh Mahal	25 C3	Telibara	31 C4	Yamuna Vihar	30 B2 30 BC2
Sheikh Sarai Ph. I	41 A4	Teliwara	24 A1	Yograj Clny.	29 C1
Sherpur	30 A1	Thakkar Bapa Nagar	22 Ab2	Zakir Nagar	44 Bc2
Shiv Nagar	36 C1	Than Singh Nagar	22 B1	Zamrudpur	41 B3
Shiv Shakti Vihar	32 C2	Tigri Clny.	42 A2		
Shiv Vihar	30 C1	Tigri Extn.	42 A2	**AIRLINES**	
Shivaji Nagar	50 B2	Tigri	42 A2	Delta Airlines	20 A2
Shivaji Park Clny.	51 A3	Tihar	36 C1	Indian Airlines	48 B1 49 B3
Shivaji Park	31 C3	Tilak Khand	45 A4	Sahara India	41 C4
Shivpuri	34 A2 37 B4 50 A1	Tis Hazari	24 A1	Thai Airways	41 C3
Shri Ram Colony	30 A1	Tughlaqabad Extn.	42 BC1		
Shri Ram Nagar	31 C4	Tughlaqabad Institutional Area	42 AB2	**AUDITORIUM**	
Shyam Enclave	34 Bc1	Tughlaqabad	42 C2	Ambedkar Youth Centre	32 A1
Shyam Nagar	45 B4	Tukmirpur	30 A1	Auditorium	49 A3
Shyam Park	32 C2	Tunda Nagar	30 C1	Diwan Hall	25 C2
Sibbanpura	46 A2	Turab Nagar	47 B3	Dr. MA Ansaari Auditorium	44 C2
Sidharth Enclave	44 A1	Uday Park	41 A3	Dr.Ambedkar	20 B2
Sidhartha Ext.	44 A1	Urban Estate	50 A1	Gandhi Memorial Hall	20 C1
Sidhartha Nagar	44 A1	Usha Park	36 C1	Ghalib Inst.	20 B1
Sidipura	23 D2	Uttra Khand	38 B1	Kamani	20 B2
Sihani Kalan	46 A1	Vaishal	33 A4	LTG	20 B2
Silampur Colony	31 Ab4	Vaishali Extension	33 A4	Mavlankar Hall	20 A2
Silampur Housing Complex	31 A4	Vaishali	37 B3	Nehru Youth Centre	47 B3
Silver Park	34 A2	Varun Enclave	52 A1	Parsi Anjuman	20 C1
Siri Fort	41 AB3	Vasant Kunj	39 A3	Shankarlal Murlidhar	20 B1
Sitapuri	37 AB3	Vashisht Park	37 C3	Siri Fort	41 A3
Sitaram Bazar	25 C3	Vasundhara Enclave	52 A1	Tagore Hall	20 C2
Slum Colony	26 A2	Vasundhara	33 B3	Teen Murti Bhawan	18 C1
Soami Nagar North	41 AB4	Vayusenabad	42 A2	Vigyan Bhawan	21 A3
Soami Nagar South	41 AB4	Vigyan Vihar	34 C1	Vivekanand	34 C1
Som Vihar	19 A4	Vijay Enclave	37 B3	World Trade Tower	20 B1
Sonia Vihar	30 A1	Vijay Ghat	25 D2		
South Extension Part I	40 A2	Vijay Nagar Colony	47 A4	**BANKS**	
South Extension Part II	40 A2	Vijay Nagar	47 A4	Allahabad	20 A1
Sriniwaspuri	44 A2	Vijay Park	31 B3 50 B2	Andhra Bank	22 A3
Sriniwaspuri Extension	44 A2	Vijay Vihar Phase I	27 A3	Bank of Madura	23 C2
State Guest Hse. Cplx.	19 B3	Vijay Vihar Phase II	27 A3	Benaras State Bank	25 D3
Subhas Nagar	50 B1	Vikas Kunj	36 A1	Dena	22 A3
Subhash Colony	42 A1	Vikaspuri	36 A1	National Bank for Agriculture	

& Rural Dev.	20 C1	Bata	49 A4	Faridabad Indl. Assn.	49 A4
PNB.	20 A2	Bawa Potteries	39 B3	Farmtrac Division	49 C3
Punjab & Sindh	22 A3	Bee Key Motors	24 A1	Fast Foods	46 B1
Punjab Co-op.	24 B2	Betavision Electronics	52 A2	Federal Chain	33 A3
RBI	20 A2	Bhalia Motors	45 B4	Fibcom India	51 B3
SBI. HQ.	20 A1	Bharat Battery	32 C2	Flex	52 A3
UCO	20 A2	Bharti Telecom	51 A4	Floor & Furnishing	51 C3
Vaish Co-op. Bank	24 B2	Bhatia Metal Containers	32 B2	Frank House	52 A2
Vaish Co-op. New Bank	25 C3	Bichhona	33 B3	Frigorifico Allana	33 C2
		Binatone Electronics	33 A4	Galaxy Electronic	52 B1
BUS TERMINUS		Biomics	45 B4	Ganesh Paper	46 B1
Anand Vihar	34 C2	BK Steel	49 B4	Garg Associates	46 B1
DTC Bus Depot	20 C2	BKP Mediavision	52 A4	Garg Wire Products	32 B2
DTC Bus Terminal	21 C3	Black Gold	32 B2	Garland Engineers	48 A1
Rajasthan Bus Terminal	21 B3	Bludip	46 B1	Gauri	33 A3
		BPS	46 B1	GD Rathi Steels	31 C4
BUSINESS ORGANISATIONS		Brite Chemicals	33 A3	GD Steels & Gases	33 B3
Addisons Paints & Chemicals	45 B3	Calcom Electronics	45 B4	GDA Godown	47 B3
Aggarwal Oil	52 A2	Calcutta Udyog	46 B1	Ghaziabad Co	47 B4
Ahuja Radio	45 B4	Carpets	46 B1	Glaxo	45 B3 46 A1
Air Reduction	33 A3	CEC	33 A3	Glaxy Inds.	28 B3
Air Tel	51 A4	Central Ware Housing Corpn.	51 A3	GM MTNL	45 A3
Ajudhia Textiles	28 A2	Centre for Dev. of Telematics	22 B3	GN Engrs.	48 A1
Alaska	45 B4	Champion	33 A3	Godrej & Boyce	46 B1
Albert David	46 B1	Chaudhary Hammer	46 B2	Golden Proteins	33 B3
Alfa Automobiles	48 B2	Competent Automobiles	39 C4	Gopal Paper & Board	46 B1
Allena Auto	28 A3	Continental Leather	45 B4	Goushala	39 B4
Alliance Boards	32 A2	Cranex Ltd.	33 A3	Grace Furnishing	33 B3
Allied Group	52 A2	Crompton Greeves	32 A2	Grace	33 B3
Allied Nippon	33 C3	Cryogenics	33 B3	Green Field Processed Foods	50 C2
Alok	33 A3	DD Gears	28 B3	Gupta Timber	33 A3
Alwyn Refrigerator	46 A1	Deki Electronic	52 B2	Gurunanak Chemical	32 C2
Ambassador Press	45 B4	Dekora Paint	32 B2	Hada Steel Products	48 B2
Amita Indicators	32 B2	Delhi Automobiles	33 B3	Hamdard	46 B1
Amrit Banaspati	47 C4	Delhi Blue Art Pottery	19 C4	Harig India	32 C2
Anand	33 A3	Delhi Press	33 A3	HCL HP	52 A3 52 B2
Aneja Box	28 A3	Delton Cable	48 B2	Heatly & Gresham	33 A3
Aneja Printers	52 B2	Deltronix	52 C1	Helio Graphic System	33 B3
Anil Oxygen Acetylene	33 A4	Dewan Rubber	46 B1	Hero HondaMotors	51 A4
Anita Die Casting	28 A3	DFM Foods	46 A2	HGB Precision Compts.	32 C2
Anu Products Ltd.	48 C1	Digi Pulse	51 A4	Himalaya Handloom	46 A2
AOT	33 A3	Dior	33 B3	Hind	33 A3
Apollo Corporate Office	51 C3	Disco Bright Bars	46 B1	Hindustan Lever	32 C1
Apparel Express	45 B4	Divine Compressor	48 A2	Hindustan Monark	46 B1
Apt. Engg.	28 A3	Dixon	52 C1	Hindustan Tin	47 B4
Ar Dee BPL Refrigerator	46 A1	DLF Industries	49 B4	Home Appliances	33 B3
Arora Soap	32 C2	Eaco Labs	52 A3	Hotline Wittis	51 A4
Asean Brown Boveri	49 A4	East India Udyog	32 A2	Hyderabad Allwyn	22 A1
Ashnoor Textile	51 A4	Eastern Silk Inds.	52 A3	Ice Factory	23 D1 48 B1 48 C1
Ashok Oil	46 B1	ECE	46 B2	ICGEB	39 B3
Ashoka Metal Decor	26 B1	Eicher Tractors Depot	47 C4	ICSSR	39 B3
Asian Paint	33 A3 46 B1	Ekta Rubber	32 A2	IDL Chemicals	33 A3
Atex Exports	51 B3	ELF Lubricants	46 B1	Indian Cottage Industries	39 C3
Atlas Cycles	33 A3	Escorts Yamaha	49 B4	Indian Glass	33 B3
Auto Gears	33 B3	Escorts Tractors	49 C3	Indian Handicraft Emporium	39 C3
Auto Meters	52 A3	Escorts	49 B3	Indl. Work Centre	27 A4
Avery India	48 A1	ESS Aar Motors	23 D3	Indo Asian	45 B4
Bajaj Mechanicals	45 B3	Essar Steel	49 A4	Indo Carpet	39 C3
Balaji Estate	45 A4	Essel Studio	52 A4	Indraprastha Cold Storage	28 A2
Bansilal	32 C2	Ester Chemicals	32 C2	Indts. Dept.	28 A3
Bareja Pumps	51 A3	Excel	28 A3	Indu Timber	32 B2
Barmalt	51 C3	Falcon	42 A3	Indure	33 B3

Name	Code	Name	Code	Name	Code
Inteecon India	52 C1	Mehtab Potteries	50 C1	Prime Steels	33 A3
Jackson Engrs	52 B1	Metal Engineering	49 A4	Prince	52 B2
Jagjit	32 C2	Metro Motors	52 A3	Progressive Instruments	32 B2
Jai Enterprise	32 B2	Metro Refrigeration	46 B1	P-Tex	33 A3
Jai Mata Ply Wood	33 B3	Mevitee	33 B3	Punj Sons	45 A4
Jain Hosiery India	53 A3	Micro Engg.	51 A3	Punjab Stainless Steel	28 A3
Jain Textile	51 A4	Miglani	30 C1	Punjab Steel	33 A3
Jamal Carpets	39 C3	Minda Switch	52 A2	Quality Enterprises	46 A1
Janta Engg. Works	32 C2	MK Overseas	33 A3	RA Nariman Singar	28 A3
Jayaar Solar	33 A4	Modern Industries	32 C2	Rachna Metal	33 A3
Jayanita Exports	32 B2	Modern Steel	46 B1	Radiant Polymers	33 A3
Jayco Pipes	33 B3	Modi Earth Mover	51 A4	Rajdhani Leasing	32 C2
Jayna Time	32 B2 32 C2	Modi Flour Mills	45 B3	Rajdhani Paints	47 C4
Jaypee Spintex	52 A2	Modi Motors	51 A3	Rama Cables	45 B4
Jhalani Tools	49 A4	Modi Xerox	45 B4	Rana Steel nTube	33 B3
JHS Electronics	51 A4	Mohan Meakins	47 B4	Ranjay Solvis	50 B1
Jims	26 B2	Moon Beverages	33 A3	Rapid Roto	33 C3
JJ Export Import	45 B4	Moser Bayer India	52 B3	Raptaka	33 B3
JJC	27 B4	MRG	52 A2	Rashtriya Sahara	52 B2
Johnson Pedder	47 A3	Nagar Electronics	51 A4	Rasik Plast	52 B2
Jugnu	52 A3	Narain	48 A1	Rastogi Engg.	33 A3
Jupitar	33 B3	National Cables	52 A3	Ravimex	33 B3
Kalinga Udyog	32 C2	National Iron & Steel	45 A3	Rawal Automobiles	47 C4
Karan Press	45 B4	National Small Industries Corp.	45 A3	Rice Mill	26 A2
Kay Aar Biscuits	46 B1	National Textiles	49 A4	Ritikas Intl.	45 B4
KC Textile	28 B3	Neeru Steel Tubes	33 B3	Rock Well Electronics	32 B2
Kelvinator Compressors	49 A4	NFDC	45 A4	Rockwin Flowmeter	32 B2
Kesaria Rubber	50 B1	NICFS	27 B4	Rohit Steel & Forgings	32 B2
Key Tee	52 A2	Nisha Optical	32 B2	Rose Impex	45 B4
Kisan Motors	46 A2	Nitco Roadways	32 A2	Rotomac Elecs.	32 B2
KNG Bearings	32 A2	Nulon India	52 A2	Royal Coatings	33 A3
Komex Foods	46 B1	Numero Uno	45 B4	RR Exports	43 A3
Konark TV	52 A2	Olympic Rubber	32 B2	RR Foundary	30 B1
Kothari Pouches	52 A3	Onida Savak	52 A2	SAB Electronics	33 A3
KTI	52 A4	Onida	45 B4	Sadhna Foundry	46 B1
Kumar Printers	45 B4	Orien	33 B3	Sagar Manthan Hitashi	52 C1
Lakshmi Video Studio	52 A4	Oshu	39 C3	Sage Metal	33 B3
Larsen & Toubro	49 A4	Paam	52 A3	Sahibabad Engg. Works	32 C2
Laxmi Traders	32 A2	Pace Marketing	32 C2	Salora TV	52 A3
Lipton	47 C4	Paharpur	33 B3	Sanskriti Apparels	51 A3
Living Media India	52 B1	Paper Coaters	32 A2	Saraswati Indl. Syndicate	52 C2
Lumax	28 A3	Paras Milk	33 A3	Savita Steel	33 B3
Luxor Pen	45 B3	Parishudh Sadhan	46 A2	Saya Automobiles	28 B3
Luxor	45 B3	Paul Chemical	32 C2	Secur	32 B2
Madras Soap Mill	28 A3	PCS Data General	52 B2	Sethi Industrial Products	48 C1
Magnum Papers	33 A3	Pearl Global	51 C3	Shakuntla Steel	47 C4
Maharaja Refractories	47 C4	Peico Electronics	32 A2	Shalimar Paints	50 C2
Maharaja Whiteline	51 C3	Pentagon	33 C3	Shankar Gold Store	47 C4
Mahaveer Cylinders	32 C2	PGCL	32 A2	Shastri Opthalmic Glassing	50 A2
Maiden Circuit	52 A2	Pharma	33 B3	Shipra	33 B3
Malviya Chemicals	33 A3	Phoenix Overseas	52 A3	Shree Mahadev Agencies	52 B2
Manu Chemicals	32 C2	Phoenix	52 A3	Shree Motors	49 A4
Marvil Vinyls	33 A3	Pick up Electronics	33 B3	Shreetron Screen	32 B2
Marwah Films & Video Studio	52 A4	Pik India	50 A2	Shyam Garments	33 A3
Mascot	46 B1	Pioneer Paper	32 C2	Sigma Rubber	28 A3
Masudpur Dairy Farm	39 A3	Plastics & Chemicals	45 B4	Silver Star	52 A2
Mayur Glass	52 A2	Polar	52 A2	Sinter Kings Virmani	28 A3
MB Rubber	32 C2	Polyplex Corpn.	51 A4	SK Marble	49 B4
MCD	27 B3	Prakash Electronics	45 B4	SLP Controller	48 A2
MCE Products	33 A4	Prakash Pipes	52 B2	Smita Conductors	47 B4
Mechanical Works	46 B1	Prasad Production Studio	52 A4	Software Tech. Park	45 A3
Mechino Polymer	51 A4	Premier Compts.	45 B3	Soma Plumbing Fixtures	33 A4

Name	Ref	Name	Ref	Name	Ref
Sona Paints	32 B2	Usha Mill	33 A3	Raj	50 C1
Sonex	52 C1	Utlam Sucootech	46 A2	Regal	20 A1
Spark Engg.	33 B3	Vama	52 B1	Ritz	24 B1
Spartan Paints	45 B4	Vegepro Foods & Feeds	52 A3	Rivoli	20 A1
Spectrum Coatings	50 C2	Venus Indl. Corpn.	51 A4	Sagar	48 B1
SR Enterprises	51 A3	Victors Cables	32 B2	Sangam	19 A4
SRB Machines	32 B2	Videocon	46 B1	Sangam	30 C1
Sri Ganesh Research Inst.	46 B1	Vigsons Automobiles	47 B3	Sapna	41 C3
SS Engg. Inds.	52 A2	Vijay Dying	51 A4	Satyam	30 C1
ST Micro Electronics	52 A4	Vijay Power Generators	52 A2	Shakuntalam Theatre	20 C2
Standard Rubber	51 A3	Vijay Prints	32 B2	Shalimar	44 A1
Standuel Potteries	39 B3	Vikas Exports	51 A4	Shiela	24 A3
Steel Fabs	32 B2	Vipul Motors	48 A2	Shringar Theatre	20 C2
Structural Water Proofing	52 A3	Virk India	52 A2	Stadium	21 B3
Studio Kabuki Romesh Film	52 A4	VKay Polymers	39 B4	Sudarshan	40 A2
Subrose	52 A2	Wadco Tools	33 A3	Swarn	34 B1
Sudershan Cold Storage	28 A1	Wall Boards & Laminates	33 A3	Triveni Theatre	20 B1
Sunbeam Rubber	50 A2	Wardex	32 BC2Pharm.	Urvashi	46 A2
Sundew Chemical	33 B3	Welding& Belting	47 B4	Virat	42 A1
Super Cassette	52 A3	Weston	52 C1	Westend	24 A2
Super Snacks	46 B1	Wood Craft	52 B3		
Super Time	52 A2	Yogindra Earth Mover	51 B3	**CIRCLES & JUNCTIONS**	
Suprion	33 A3			Ajronda Chk.	49 B3
SW Rubber Works	46 B1	**CINEMA**		Ashram Chowk	44 A1
Swadesh Polytex	47 C3	Ajit	50 C1	Ayodhya Chowk	27 B3
Swadeshi Fan	52 B2	Aradhana	32 A2	Basai Chk.	50 A2
Swama Motors	24 A1	Baldev	49 A4	Bata Chk.	49 A4
Switching System	51 A4	Basant	46 B2	Bhajanpura Chowk	30 A2
System Controls & Transformers	46 B1	Chanakya	19 B3	Chhatta Chowk	25 C2
Tata Export	45 B4	Chowdhary	47 B4	Chitli Qabar Chowk	25 C3
Tata Oil Mills	32 C1	Dev	50 C1	Dayal Chk.	23 C3
Tata Pipes	32 A2	Dharm Palace	52 A4	DC Chowk	26 C2
TCI	32 A2	Eros	40 C1	Deepali Chowk	27 C4
Telco	33 A3	Excelsior	24 B2	Dholi Piao Chk.	36 A1
Telemats Servo	33 A3	Filmistan	23 D2	Dispensary Chowk	30 A2
Teletube Electronics	47 C3	Gagan	49 A4	Durga Chowk	26 A2
Thapar Plaza	47 B4	Gianand	31 C4	Durgapuri Chowk	31 C3
Thomson Press	49 B3	Golcha	25 C3	Faiz Chk.	23 C3
Tool Mak	33 A3	Hamsadhwani Theatre	20 C2	Fatehpuri Chowk	24 B2
Track Pack India	52 B1	Jagat	25 C3	Fawdha Singh Chk.	49 A4
Trading Engg.	28 A3	Janak	37 B3	Fountain Chk.	50 B2
Transport Centre	32 A2	Jay	50 A1	Ghonda Chowk	31 B3
Transport Corpn. of India	48 B2	Kavita Palace	30 C1	Guru Teg Bahadur Chk.	29 D3
Tricolit	33 A3	Liberty	22 B2	Hauz Qazi Chowk	24 B3
Tristar	46 B1	Manoher	47 A3	Idgah Chk.	23 D2
Uni Air Refrigeration	52 A3	Meenakshi Palace	30 C2	Jheel Chk.	34 A1
Unichem Labs	46 B1	Minerva	25 C1	Kalyan Singh Chk.	49 A4
Uniplas	52 A2	Mohan Chitralok	47 B3	Karkar Duma Chk.	34 B2
United Deco	32 B2	Moti	25 C2	Lajwanti Garden Chk.	36 C2
United Pressure Cooker	28 A3	Navrang	47 B4	Lal Bahadur Shastri Chk.	48 C2
United Television	52 B2	Neelam	49 A3	Madhuban Chk.	35 A3
Universal Fasteners	48 B2	New Amar	24 B3	Mandi House Chk.	20 B2
Universal Glass	33 A3	Novelty	24 A1	Mati Dass Chowk	24 B2
Universal Tube	33 B3	Odeon	20 A1	Motilal Nehru Place	21 A3
UP Ceramics & Potteries	47 C4	Palace	23 D1	Neelam Chk.	49 A3
UP State Warehouse	33 B3	Paras	41 C4	Netaji Chk.	32 C1
Upica Polyrin	33 A3	Pawan	47 B4	Rajiv Gandhi Chk.	48 A1 51 B3
Uptron Colour Tubes	32 C2	Plaza	20 A1	Rohitash Nagar Chowk	31 C4
Uptron Service	32 A2	Race Course	18 C2	Sai Baba Chowk	27 C3
Urdu & Multi Language Software		Rachna	22 A3	Shankaracharya Chowk	24 A1
Development Centre	20 B1	Radhu Palace	35 A3	Sherpur Chowk	30 A1
Usha Electronics	52 A2	Radhu	31 C4	Shiv Vihar Chowk	30 B1

Sihani Chowk	46 A1	Angola	18 A1	Russia	18 B2
Vishram Chowk	27 B3	Australia	18 B2	Rwanda	40 A2
Windsor Place	20 A2	Austria	18 A2	San Marino	21 A4
		Bangladesh	40 C2	Saudi Arabia	40 A2

CLUBS / MEMBERSHIP INSTITUTIONS

Air Beam Club	29 D2	Belgium	19 A3	Serbia & Montenegro	18 B2
Aravali Club	49 B4	Bhutan	19 A3	Seychelles	39 C3
Arun Vihar Inst. Club	52 B4	Brazil	21 A3	Singapore	19 A3
Bata Club	49 A4	Bulgaria	18 A2	Somalia	40 B1
Bengali Club	24 B1	Cambodia	41 A4	Spain	21 A4
Boat Club	20 A2 36 C1	Canada	18 B2	Sri Lanka	18 B1
Central Lib.	42 B2	China	18 B1	Sudan	18 B2
Central Secretariat Lib.	19 A4	Congo	41 B4	Sweden	18 A2
Chelmsford Club	20 A2	Costa Rica	40 B2	Switzerland	18 AB2
Children's Riding Club	18 C2	Croatia	40 C2	Tajikistan	44 B2
Citizen's Club	50 C1	Czech & Slovakia	19 B3	Thailand	18 A2
Club	18 A2 19 A4 50 B2	Denmark	21 A4	The Republic of Korea	18 A2
Delhi Commonwealth		Egypt	19 B3	Togo	45 B3
Women Assn.	41 B3	Estonia	41 C3	Turkey	19 A3
Delhi Flying Club	19 C3	Ethiopia	19 B3	United Arab Emirates	18 A2
Delhi Gliding Club	19 C3	European Community	21 B4	United Kingdom	18 B2
Delhi Golf Club	21 B4	Finland	18 B2	United States of America	18 B2
Delhi Gymkhana Club	18 C2	France	18 B2	Uzbekistan	18 A2
Delhi Public Library	19 B3 44	Georgia	41 B3	Venezuela	41 A4
	A2 20 B2 22 B1 24 B1	Germany	18 B2	Vietnam	18 B1
Delhi Race Club	18 C2	Ghana	19 A3		
Delhi Tamil Sangam	19 A4	Greece	21 C3	**EDUCATIONAL INSTITUTIONS**	
District Library	49 C3	Grenada	21 C3	Acharya Narendra Dev College	45 A4
Faridabad Swimming &		Hungary	19 B3	Adarsh Pub. Sch.	36 A1
Health Club	48 C1	Indonesia	18 B1	Admn. Staff College of India	38 A2
GBET Pub. Lib.	49 A4	Iran	20 B1	Advance Medical Technology	27 B4
GDA Club	46 C2	Israel	21 A4	Agriculture Edn. Ctr.	51 B3
Gymkhana Club	48 B2	Italy	18 A2	All India Inst. of Chartered	
Gymnasium	38 B2	Japan	18 B2	Surveyors	32 A2
Hardayal Municipal		Jordan	21 B4	All India Ophthalmological Society	34 B2
Corporation Library	24 B2	Korea (DPR)	44 A2	Amar Nath DAV Sch.	51 A3
Health Club	49 C3	Kuwait	19 B3	Ambedkar Vocational Trg. Ctr.	43 A3
Holiday Club	41 B4	Kyrgyzstan	19 B4	American Inst. of Indian Studies	51 C3
Library	19 A4 23 D3 29 D2 38 B2	Laos	44 A1-2	Anchal & Pavaan Schools	
Medical Lib.	19 C4	Latvia	18 A1	for Disabled Children	18 B1
National Medical Library	40 A2	Lebanon	18 A1 18 B1	Andhra Hs. Sch.	20 C1
National Sports Club of India	20 C2	Libya	21 B4	Andrews Scots Sch.	35 B3
Netaji Sports Club	40 B1	Lithuania	41 B3	Angles Pub. Sch.	48 A1
New Friends Club	44 B2	Luxembourg	41 B3	Anglo Arabic Sch.	24 B3
Press Club of India	20 A2	Malaysia	19 B3	Anglo Indian Pub. Sch.	29 D1
Railway Club	19 B3	Malta	20 A2	Annamalai University	42 A2
Residents Club	50 A1	Mauritius	18 A2 18 B1	Anupam Inst. of Management	50 A2
Rotary Club	47 B3	Mongolia	21 B4	Apeejay Sch.	49 B3 49 C3 41 A4
Safdarjung Club	19 C4	Morocco	21 B4	Aptech	49 A3 52 A4
South Delhi Club	41 B3	Myanmar	18 B2	Arab Cultural Centre	18 A2
Sports Club	29 C3	Nauru	41 B4	Army Pub. Sch.	52 B4
Sports Cultural Club	44 A2	Nepal	20 B2	Art Institution	44 C2
Tennis Association	38 C1	Netherlands	18 B2	Arts & Commerce Col.	19 A3
Tennis Club	24 B1	New Zealand	19 A3	Arunudaya Public Sch.	34 B2
Yoga Centre	40 B2	Nicaragua	21 A4	Arya Bhat Polytechnic	28 B3
Youth Club	40 A1	Norway	18 B1	Assisi Convent Sch.	52 C2
Zim Health Club	49 B3 49 C4	Pakistan	18 B2	Auxilium HS Sch.	19 A4
		Panama	40 B2	Ayurvedic Research Centre.	37 C4
DIPLOMATIC MISSIONS		Peru	44 A2	Bagrodia Pub. Sch.	27 C3
Afghanistan	18 B2	Philippines	19 A3	Bal Bhawan Pub. Sch.	35 C4
Algeria	19 B4	Poland	19 B3	Bhai Parmanand Instn.	
		Portugal	21 C3	of Business Studies	35 A3
		Qatar	18 A2	Bharat Scouts & Guides	

Name	Ref
Trg. Centre	21 C4 23 C1
Bharati Pub. Sch.	52 B3
Bharti Mahila College	36 B2
Bharti Mahila Col.	23 C3
Bharti Public SS Sch.	35 B3
Bhatnagar International Sch.	39 A3
Bidhan Chandra Vidyalaya	19 A3
Blind Sch.	21 C4
Blue Bells	41 B3
Boys & Girls SS Sch.	41 A4
Boys SS Sch.	34 A2
British Sch.	18 A2
Cambridge Sch.	52 B4
Cambridge SS Sch.	52 B4
Cambridge	40 C2
Carmel Convent	18 B1
Central Road Research Institute	45 B3
Chawan Rishi Intl.	51 C3
Chinmaya	38 A1
Col. of Art	20 B2
College of Engg. Management & Tech.	32 B2
College of Management Technology	46 B1
College of Pharmacy	42 B2
DAV Inst. of Management & Vocational Studies	32 B1
DAV PG College	40 C2
DAV Pub. Sch.	27 B4 39 A3-4 45 A3 48 C2
DAV Sch.	19 A4 29 D3 34 A1 34 C2
DAV SS Sch	25 C3
DAVSS Sch.	23 C3
Dayal Singh Col.	21 B4
Dayanand Pub. HS	48 C1
Dayanand Pub. Sch.	49 A3
DCM HS.Sch.	23 C2
Deen Dayal Research Inst.	23 D3
Delhi Council for Child Welfare	37 C3 42 A2
Delhi Inst. of Technology	25 C1
Delhi Kannada Tech. Inst.	21 B4
Delhi Pub. Sch.	46 B1
Delhi Public Sch.	19 A4 52 B3 21 C4 41 C3 48 A1
Deshbandhu College	45 A4
Deta SS. Sch.	21 B4
Dharam Pub. Sch.	52 C2
Dinanath Pub. Deg. Col.	49 A3
Dist. Edn. & Trg. Ctr.	50 B2
Dist. Edn. Trg. Ctr.	48 B1
District Inst. of Edn. & Trg.	19 A3
Don Bosco Sch.	42 B1
Don Bosco Technical Institute	45 B3
Dronacharya College	50 B1
Dwarka Pub. Sch.	37 A4
Eclat Academy	22 A3
Edn. Research Ctr.	50 B2
Engg. & Technology Faculty	44 C2
Engineering Service Centre	38 B2
Faculty of Islamic Studies	42 B2
Faith Academy	22 A2
Faridabad Productivity Council	48 C1
Father Agnal Sch.	40 A2
Fatima Convent	50 A1
Fatima ConventJr. Sch.	50 C1
Fine Arts	44 C2
Food Craft Inst.	40 C2
Foot Wear Design & Development Institute	52 A3
Foreign Languages Sch.	21 A4
Forma's Maritime Inst.	38 C2
Foundation for Applied Research in Cancer	38 C2
Frank Anthony pub. Sch.	40 B2
Gandharwa Sangeet College	47 B3
Gargi College	41 A3
GB Pant Polytechnic	45 B4
GD Goenka Pub. Sch.	39 A3
Geeta Sanjay Mem Pub. Sch.	46 B2
Geetanjali Pub. Sch.	30 A2
Giri Pub. Sch.	45 C4
Girl's SS Sch.	23 C2 23 C3
Girls SS Sch.	34 A2
Golden Jubilee Sch.	50 C1
Goverdhan Vidya Niketan	31 C3
Govt Girl's SS Sch.	23 D3
Govt Girl's SS. Sch.	20 A1 41 C4
Govt Girl's SS Sch.	23 D2
Govt. Boys SS Sch.	19 B4 34 A2 36 B2 42 A1 44 A1
Govt. Boys SS Sch.	37 C4
Govt. Degree College	48 B2 50 C1 52 A3
Govt. Girls College	48 B2
Govt. Girls SS Sch.	19 A3 25 C2 36 B2 36 C141 A3 42 A2 44 A1 45 A4 48 B1 49 A3 49 A4
Govt. H Sch.	43 A348 A1
Govt. High Sch.	51 C3 51 C4
Govt. Motor Driving Trg. Ctre.	30 C2
Govt. S Sch.	34 C2
Govt. Sch.	34 C1 35 C3
Govt. SS Sch.	19 A4 29 D3 30 A1 34 A1 35 A3 35 B3 35 B4 35 C4
Govt. Vocational Edn. Institute	48 B1
Great Mary Pub. Sch.	36 A2
Green Fields Sch.	19 B4
Greh Kalyan Kendra	19 A3
Guru Gobind SingIndraprastha University	25 C1
Guru Harikrishan Pub. Sch.	31 C3
Guru HK Pub. Sch.	34 B2
Guru Nanak Co-Education Polytechnic	26 C1
Gyanand Vidya Bhandar	30 B2
Hamdard Pub. Sch.	43 B3
Happy Model Sch.	36 B1
Happy Vidyalaya	25 C3
Haryard Sch.	34 B2
Hemant High Sch.	47 B3
Hi Tech. Vocatioanl Trg. Ctr.	42 C1
Himalayan Pub. Sch.	27 C3
Hindi Academy	23 C1
Hindon Pub. Sch.	32 C1
Holy Angels Sch.	32 C1
Holy Child Sch.	47 B3
Holychild Pub. Sch.	48 A1
HS Sch.	32 A1
Human Resources Development Institution	52 A4
IBP Trg. College	52 C4
IG Inst. of Physical Edn. & Sports Sciences	36 A1
Indian Council of Edn.	19 B4
Indian Inst. of Packaging	23 D3
Indian Inst. of Forein Trade	38 C2
Indian Inst. of Hardware Tech.	36 A1
Indian Inst. of Public Administration	20 C1
Indian Institute of Technology	38 C1
Indian Instituteof Mass Communication	38 B2
Indian Law Inst.	20 B2
Indian National Pub. Sch.	52 B3
Indian National Scientific Documentation	38 B2
Indian Society of Technical Edn.	38 C2
Indian Statistical Institute	38 C2
Indl. Trg.Institute	50 C1
Industrial Training Institute	48 A2
Industrial Trg. Institute	48 B1
Ingraham Institute	46 C2
Inst of Management Studies	47 C3
Inst. of Applied Manpower Research.	20 C1
Inst. of Archaeology	20 C2
Inst. of Beauty Culture & Health	46 C2
Inst. of Chartered Accountants	52 A2
Inst. of Company Secrataries	22 A3
Inst. of Indian Foundrymen	42 A2
Inst. of Interactual Property Research & Practice	51 C3
Inst. of Management Technology	46 C2
Inst. of Mktg. Management	21 B4
Inst. of Russian Studies	38 C1
Inst. of Secretariat Trg. & Management	38 C1
Inst. of Surveyors	38 C2
Inst. ofHome Economics	40 A2
Institute of Manpower Research	44 A1
Institute of Pathology	19 C4
Inter College	47 A3
International Studies	38 B2
Italian Cultural Centre	18 A2
ITI	29 D2 34 A1 36 B1 36C2
Jack & Jil Play Sch.	33 BC1
Jagan Institute of Management	26 B2
Jagjivan Ram Sch.	32 C2
Jagjivan Ram Vidya Bvn.	23 C3
Jain Vidyalaya	25 D3
Jamia Hamdard University	42 B2
Jamia Teachers Col.	45 C3
Janki Devi Girl's Col.	23 C3
Jawaharlal Nehru National Youth Centre	52 B1
Jawaharlal Nehru	

Name	Ref
University	38 B2 38 B1 38 B2
Jesus & Mary College	18 A2
Jijabai ITI for Women	41 A3
Jindal Pub. Sch.	37 B3
JKG College	47 A4
Junior Navyug Sch.	19 A3
Kalindi Col.	22 A3
Kalka Pub. Sch.	42 B1
Kamla Nehru College	41 A3
Kendriya Bhandar	38 A1 41 B3
Kendriya Vidyalaya	34 B2 34 C1 36 B2 38 B1 38 B2 40 A1 40 B2 41 A3 44 B2
Kerala Sch.	36 A1
Kerala SS. Sch.	20 B2
Khaitan Pub. Sch.	52 C4
Khalsa Col & Sch.	22 B2
Khalsa College	29 D3
Khalsa Sch.	40 C2
Khalsa	40 A1
KL Mehta Dayanand Pub. Sch.	48 B2 49 A3
Lady Hardinge Medical Col.	20 A1
Lady Irwin SS. Sch.	20 A2
Lady Irwin Col.	20 B2
Lady Reading Health Sch.	23 D1
Lady Shri Ram College for Women	41 B3
Lajpat Rai College	32 C2
Lakshmi Bai Batra Nursing School	42 B2
Lakshmi Mahavidyalaya	20 C3
Lal Bahadur Shastri Sanskrit Vidyapith	38 C2
Lal Bahadur Shastri SS Sch.	38 C1
Lions Vidya Mandir	18 C1
Little Infants Montessori	39 A4
Lord Mahavir Sch.	52 B4
Mahadev Desai SS Sch.	48 B2
Maharaja Surajmal Institution	36 B2
MaharanaMemorial Pub. Sch.	50 C1
Maitreyi College	18 A2
Malaria Research Centre	29 D2
Manav Bharti International Sch.	41 A4
Masonic Pub. Sch.	39 A3
Mass Communication & Research Centre	45 C3
Mata Gujri Pub. Sch.	29 D3
Mata Sundari Women's Col.	20 B1
Mater Dei Sch.	20 B2
Maulana Azad Medical Col.	20 BC1
MCD Boys Sch.	36 C1
Meera Polytechnic	44 A1
Mira Model Sch.	36 B1
MM Harijan College	47 B4
Modern Sch. & Women Polytechnic	52 B2
Modern Sch.	21 B3 48 C2 20 B1
Modern Vidya Niketan S. Sch.	48 C2
Mohta Inst. of Management	49 A3
Montessori Sch.	29 D2
Mota Singh SS Sch.	36 A2
Mother Divine Pub. Sch.	27 B3
Mother Teresa SS Sch.	35 B3
Mt. Abu SS Sch	27 B3
Nagraj Spritual Centre	35 B3
Nari Niketan	36 C2
National Inst. of Finance	38 C1
National Inst. of Health & Family Welfare	38 B1
National Inst. of Immunology	38 B2
National Inst. of Personal Management	49 A3
National Inst. of Science	20 C1
National institute of Technology	27 B4
National Labour Institute	52 C2
National Open Sch.	50 C1
National Victor Public Sch.	35 C3
Nav Jiwan Pub. Sch.	49 C4
Nav Yug Sch.	19 B4
Naval Sch.	19 B3
Navjeevan Pub. Sch.	29 D3
Navyug Sch.	20 A2
Navyug	40 A1
Nehru Samaj Sewa Kendra	39 C4
New Bal Bharti	27 B3
New Greenfield Pub. Sch.	42 B1
Nirmal ShikshaKendra	21 B3
NTPC	52 C2
Oriental Staff Training College	49 B4
Pitman Shorthand Sch.	22 B2
Pitmans Shorthand Institute	50 A1
Plato Pub. Sch.	35 C3
Polytechnic	44 C2
Pooma Parjana Pub. Sch.	39 A4
Pratibha Vikas Vidyalaya	26 B1 34 C1
Preet Public Sch.	35 B3
Presentation Convent	25 C2
Priya Research Centre	42 A2
Protoype Development & Training Centre NSIC	45 AB4
Psychic Spiritual Research Institute	18 B1
Punjabi Academy	23 D3
Rainbow Eng. Sch.	36 B2
Raj Kumari Amrit Kaur Nursing College	40 B2
Rajdhani Pub. Sch.	30 B1 43 A3
Rama Krishna Pub. Sch.	48 B1
Ramjas HS. Sch.	22 B2 23 D3
Ramjas Sch. Junior Wing	22 A2
Ramjas SS Sch.	22 A2
Ramjas Vidyalaya	25 D3
Ratna Devi Girls SS Sch.	34 A1
Rayan International	26 A1
Rockland Medium Sch.	48 B2
Rosary Pub. Sch.	29 C1 29 D1
Rose Land Pub. Sch.	51 A4
Rufaida Nursing Sch.	42 B2
Rural Development & Self Employment Trg. Inst.	50 A1
Ryan International Sch.	48 A1 27 C4
Sachdeva Public Sch.	26 C2
Salwan Sch.	22 B3
Sanatan Dharam S Sch.	50 A2 40 C2
Sanjay Gandhi Memorial Trust	18 B1
Sanskriti Civil Services Sch.	18 A2
Sant Nirankari Pub. Sch.	48 B1
Sant Nirankari SS Sch.	23 D3 29 D1
Saraswati Bal Mandir SS Sch.	36 C1
Saraswati Vidya Mandir	32 C1
Sardar Patel Vidyalaya	21 B4
Sarvodaya Girls Sch.	37 C4
Sarvodaya Kanya Vidyalaya	27 A4 44 B2
Sarvodaya KanyaVidyalaya	37 C3
Sarvodaya Vidyalaya	19 A4 27 B3 27 B4 27 C4 40 B2 41 C4
Sarvodya Vidyalaya	24 B1
Satyanam Pub. Sch.	43 A3
Satyawati College	28 C3
Satyawati	30 C2
SB Arya Sch.	23 C3
Seth Mukandial Inter College	46 A2
Sevti Devi Memorial Sch.	37 B3
Shiksha Kendra	35 B3
Shikshak Sadan	34 C1
Shiv Vani Model Sch.	37 A4
Shri Guru Nanak Girls Inter College	46 B2
Shri Satya Sai Vidya Vihar Sch.	42 C1
Shyama Prasad Vidyalaya	21 B4
Shyamlal College	31 C4
Sidhartha Intl. Pub. Sch.	32 B2
Small Industries Service Institute	45 A3
Somer Ville Sch.	52 C2
SS Govt Sch.	22 B2
St. Crispins SS Sch.	50 B2
St. John	41 B4
St. Mark SS Sch.	36 A2
St. Michael's Sch.	50 A1
St. Michael's SS Sch.	50 A1
St. Thomas Sch.	22 B3 32 C1
St. Xaviers Pub. Sch.	52 C4
St.Lawrence Edn. Society	26 A1
Sulabh Pub. Sch.	37 A4
Summer Field	41 B3
Sunrise Sch.	32 B1
Surya Inst.	52 C2
Tagore International Sch.	41 C3
Takshila Public Sch.	31 C3
Teachers Training Inst.	40 C2
Tech Education Ctre.	30 B2
The American Embassy Sch.	18 A2
Third World Studies	45 C3
Tibbia Col.	23 C2
Trg. Inst.	29 D2
TVB Sch.of Habitat Studies	39 A4
Tytler HS. Sch.	23 C2
Uday Bharti Pub. Sch.	48 C2
Universal Public SS Sch.	35 B3
Vanasthali Pub. Sch.	35 C3
Vidya Bhawan SS. Sch.	21 B4
Vidyawati Girls PG College	47 B3
Vikas Sadan	40 A1
Vinay Gurukul	50 A1
Vishal Pub. Sch.	48 B1
Vishwa Bharti Pub. Sch.	37 A4
Vishwa Bharti SS Sch.	52 B4

Name	Ref	Name	Ref	Name	Ref
Vishwa Yuvak Kendra	18 B1	Dist. Statistical Office	50 B2	Punjab Waqf Board	51 B3
Vivekanand Academy	50 A1	District Courts	34 B1	PWD	45 A3-4 46 B2
Vivekanand Convent	31 C3	District Office	46 C2	Pyrites Phosphates Chemical	52 C2
Vivekanand Women College	34 C1	Divisional Inspector Wildlife	48 C2	Railway Reservation Centre	34 B2
Vocational College	40 B2	DTC Printing Press	45 B3	Recruiting Office	25 C2
Vocational Edn. Inst.	50 C1	Dte. of Social Welfare	20 A2	Reg. Co-op. Sty.	20 A2
Womens Training Centre	30 B1	Dy Excise & Taxation Commn.	50 B2	Registrar General India MHA	19 A4
Women ITI	24 B1	Dy Excise and Taxation Commr.	49 C3	RTO	31 B4 36 B1 46 B2
Women Polytechnic	44 A1	Employment Exchange	24 B3	Sales Tax Office	46 C2 46 B2 47 C3
Women Technical Inst.	19 A4	ESI Corp.	20 B1	SDM Court	31 B4
Work Centre for Women	36 C2	Excise and Taxation Commissioner	49 C3	SDM's Courts	47 B4
YMCA Sewak Vocational Trg. Ctr.	49 B3	Excise Div. II	52 A4	Social Defence & Security Dept.	49 A3
Yua Shakti Model Sch.	27 B4	Export Inspection Officer	48 B1	SP's Office	48 B2
		Farmer Service Ctr.	50 C1	State Sainik Board	24 A1
GOVERNMENT OFFICES		Farmers Advisory Service Centre	51 B3	State Vigilance Bureau	50 B2
Addl. DC Police	18 B1	Fire Stn.	18 B1 19 A4	Steel Authority of India	21 B4
Afro Asian Rural Reconstruction			20 C2 24 A1 25 D3	Sub Registrar's Court	25 C3
Organisation	19 B3	Food Prodn. Research Ctr.	37 C3	Superintendent of Police	51 B3
Agricultural Finance Corp.	36 B1	Forest Office	50 B2	Supreme Court	20 C2
AICTE	20 C1	Forest Offices	48 C2	Suptdg. Engr. NH Circle	48 B1
All India Confederation		GDA Office	46 B2	Tahsil	24 A1 47 B4
of the Blind	27 B3	General Manager Data Networks	52 B2	Telecom House	51 B3
Archaeological Survey of India	21 A3	Geological Survey of India	48 A2	Telephone Customer	
Asst. Labour Commr.	45 A4	Govt. Offices	48 A2	Service Centre	26 C2
Bar Assn. of India	20 C2	Hardayal Municipal Corp. Pub. Lib.	24 A1	Textile Commr.	52 B2
BDO Office	48 B1	Haryana Agri. Dept.	51 B3	Tihar Central Jail	36 C2
CBIP	18 B1	Haryana Security & Labour Welfare Ctr.		Tis Hazari Courts	24 A1
Central Excise &		49 A4		Traffic Com. Office	30 C2
Customs	32 C1 32 C2 50 A1	Haryana Seed Development Nigam	50	Treasury Off.	50 B2 49 A3
Central Pollution Control Board	34 B1	B2		UN Military Observer Group	20 B2
Central Warehousing Corporation	52 A3	Haryana State Small Industries &		UN Offices	21 A4
Centre for Police Research	18 B1	Export Corpn.	50 C1	UNICEF	21 A4
Centre for Rly. Information System	19 A3	Horticulture Officer	48 C1	United India Insurance	48 B1 50 B2
Chief Admn. NR.	25 C1	House Tax Dept.	40 C1	UP Roadways	24 B3
Chief Planner NCR	50 A1	IG Police	19 B4	UPSC	21 B3
Collector, Customs &		Income Tax Dept.	48 A2	Weights & Measure Dept.	28 A3
Central Excise	52 B3	India Intl. Centre	21 A4		
Commissioner's Off.	50 B2 30 C2	Intensive Cattle Development		**HISTORICAL PLACES**	
Controller General		Project	51 B3	Adilabad Fort (in ruins)	43 C3
Defence Accounts	19 A4	Intl. Labour Organisation	18 B1	Ala i Minar	39 C3
Courts	49 B4	Kisan Sewa Kendra	51 A3	Amar Jawan Jyoti	21 B3
CPWD	34 B2 45 C4	Labour Officer Circle II	49 B3	Ashoka Pillar	20 C1
DC Police East	34 AB1	LIC	24 B3 47 B4	Ashokan Edict	45 A3
DDA Chief Engg.	41 A4	Marketing & InspectionDte GOI		Bara Batasha	21 C4
Delhi Bureau of Text Books	37 C3	(Agriculture)	48 A2	Bara Gumbad	21 A4
Delhi High Court	21 B3	Mini Secretariat	49 B4	Bara Khamba	21 C4
Delhi Police Training Complex	30 A1	MRTP	21 A3	Bhoori Bhatiyari	20 C1
Delhi Prisons Head Qtrs.	37 C3	Municipal Committee	50 B2	Bistdari	18 A1
Delhi Public Lib.	25 C3	Municipal Office	49 A3	Firoz Shah Kotla	20 C1
Delhi State Civil Supplies		National Archives of India	20 A2	Fort (in ruins)	42 C2
Corporation	45 C4	National Highway Authority	44 A1	Gandhi Smriti	21 A4
Delhi Stock Exchange	20 C1	National Product. Council	21 B4	Ghiyasuddin Tughlaq's Tomb	42 C2
Delhi Tourism	40 B2	NDMC. Palika Kendra	20 A1	Humayan's Tomb	21 C4
Delhi Transport Corp.	20 C2	Northern Railway HQ.	20 B2	India Gate	21 B3
DIG Police	19 A4 50 B2	NorthernRegionalElectricity Board	38 C2	Indraprastha	21 C3
Directorate of Edn.	25 D3	Oriental Insurance	37 B3 48 A1 49 A3 49 A4	Iron Pillar	39 C3
Dist. Child Welfare Board	50 A1			Isa Khan's Tomb	21 C4
Dist. Collector's Office	51 B3	Panchayat Ghar	31 A3 33 B3	Jantar Mantar	20 A1
Dist. Courts	51 B3	Passport Off.	19 A4	Khairul Manazil	21 C3
Dist. Edn. Officer	48 B2	PF Commissioner	49 B3	Khuni Darwaza	20 C1
Dist. Food Supply Corpn.	49 C4	Population Foundation of India	38 C2	Lal Bahadur Shastri Smriti	21 A3
Dist. Jail	50 B2	Power Grid Corp. of India	32 C1	Malcha Mahal	18 A1
Dist. SocialWelfare Officer	51 A3	Press Council of India	20 B2		

Mirza Ghalib	21 C4	Chawla	43 A3	Khurana	50 B2
Muhammad Shah Sayyid's Tomb	21 A4	Chuhan	52 B2	Kolmet	22 B3
Murti	18 B1	City Clinic	24 B3	Kothari	21 B4
Nai ka Kot	43 C3	Civil	50 B2	Krishna	46 A3
Purana Qila	21 C3	DAV	40 C1	Kumar	52 C1
Qutb Minar	39 C3	Dawar	50 A1	Lal Bahadur Shastri	35 C4
Safdarjang's Tomb	18 C2	Deepak	34 B2	Lala Ramswarup TB Hospital	39 C3
Salimgarh Fort	25 C1	Deepali	27 C4	Life Line	34 A2
Sundarwala Burj	21 C4	Delhi Nursing Home	30 A1	Lions	44 B2
Teen Murti	18 C1	Dharamshilla Cancer	52 A1	Madan	40 C2
Tughlaqabad Fort (in ruins)	42 BC2	Dr. Narain Chand Joshi	23 C2	Mahajan	28 A1
War Memorial Arch	21 B3	Dr. R Prasad Ctr. for Opthalmic Sciences	19 C4	Maharishi Balmiki	29 D2
HOSPITALS		Drug Relief Centre	50 B2	Majeedia	42 B2
Addi Charitable Polyclinic	52 A3	ENT	40 C1	Malhotra Heatr Inst.	40 C2
Aggarwal	49 C4 46 B2	Escorts Med. Ctr.	49 A3	Malik	52 B1
Akanksha	32 C1	Escorts	44 B2	Mamta	30 B2
Akbar	44 C2	ESI	24 B3 26 C2 27 B3 32 A1	Manglam	35 B4
All India Institute of Medical Sciences	19 C4		39 C3 47 B4 50 B2 52 C2 31 A3	Marie Stopes	27 B3
		Eye	52 B3	Mata Chanan Devi	36 A2
Amar Jayanti	41 A4	Family Planning	42 C2	Maternity Centre	31 C3
Amar Jyoti	34 C2	Friends	44 A1	Maternity Home	32 C2
Ambedkar Hospital	27 B3	Garg	27 A4 34 B2	MCD	24 B3 31 B3 40 C2 37 C4
Amit	36 C1	Gautam	28 A1	Mehar	42 A2
Anand	36 A1	Gayatri	29 C2	Mehta	49 A3
Ananda	35 B3	Gaytri	28 B2	Memorial	42 A2
Anita	32 B1	Gopal	31 C3	Metro Hospital & Heart Institute	52 B2
Arora	28 B3 49 A3	Goswami	34 C1	Mital	31 C3
Aryan	50 A1	Govt.	52 B3	Mohan	30 B2
Ashoka	34 A1	Gupta	31 C4 32 C1 36 A1 48 B1	Moll Chand	40 B2
Astha	25 C3	Guru Harkrishan	44 A1	MS	34 B2
AWHO	52 C4	Hans Charitable	29 D3	Mukundlal Municipal Govt. Hosp.	47 A3
Balaji	27 C4	Healing Home	28 B3	N. Rly.	24 A1
Banarsidas Chendiwala Eye Institute	45 B4	Health Point	43 B3	Nagia	50 B2
		Heart Institute	41 C3	Narang	28 B3
Bansal	47 B3	Holy Angels	38 B1	Narinder Mohan	47 B3
Batra	42 B2	Holy Family	44 B2	Narula	30 C2
BD Attam	28 A3	Homeopathic	41 A4	National Chest Inst.	40 A2
Bhagat	37 C3	IIT	38 C1	National Eye Bank	19 C4
Bhagwan Mahavir	27 C3	Indian Cancer Society	40 B2	Nav Jeevan	27 B4
Bhai Parmanand	29 D2	Indraprastha Apollo	45 C4	Navin Upchar Hospital	52 A4
Bhanu Eye	31 B3	Infectious Diseases	29 D2	Navjeevan	32 C1
Bhardwaj Nursing Home	52 C4	Jain	49 A3	Nawab	30 B2
Bhardwaj	52 B4	Jainak	37 AB3	Nehru Homeo College	40 B2
Bhart Ghar	40 A1	Jaipur Golden	27 B4	Noble	49 C3
Bir	36 A1	Jeevan Jyoti	36 A1 48 B2	Noida Medicare Centre	52 B4
Bishan Sarup	31 C4	Jeevan	22 B3	Noida Orthopedic Hospital	52 B3
BK	49 A3	Jeevandan	43 A3	Nulife	29 D3
BL Kapoor	22 A3	Jeewan	44 A1	Orthonova	42 A1
Blind	29 D3	Jessa Ram	22 B3	Pentamed	29 C3
Blue Bells	34 B2	Jindal	34 C2	Podar	46 B2
BR	46 B2	Joshi	27 B4	Prem Nath	50 C1
Cancer Research Centre	20 B1	Jyoti	31 C3 36 A1 50 C2	Premnath Child & Maternity	50 B2
Central	20 A1	Kailash	52 B3	Pushpanjali	51 B3
CGHS	19 A4 19 A4 36 B2 37 C3 38 C1 40 A1	Kalavani Saran Children's Hosp.	20 A1	Rachna	49 A3
		Kalra Child Care Centre	49 B3	Radhika	32 C1
Chamelidavi	32 C1	Kalyani	50 C1	Railway	20 A1 47 B3
Chandervati	48 B1	Kannu	32 B1	Rajiv Gandhi Cancer Inst.	27 B3
Chanty Birds	25 C2	Kasturba	25 C3	Rajput	30 B1
Charitable Eye	48 B1	Kaura Lal	25 C3	Ram Lal	35 B4
Chark Palika	19 A3	Kesar	37 C3	Rama	50 B2
Chaudhary	35 A4	Khatri	47 A4	Rana	30 A2
				Red Cross Drug De-	

Name	Ref
addiction Centre	49 C3
Rehabilitation Centre	26 B1
Renuka	30 C2
RK	43 B3
Ruby	31 B3
Rupali	30 C2
Safdarjang	19 C4
Sainik Sadan	40 C2
Sama	41 B3
Santosh Dental College	46 B2
Saraswati	50 C1
Saroj	27 C3
Sarvodaya	46 C2
Satya	52 B2
Sehgal	28 A1 41 BC3
Sethi	50 A2
Shankar Lal	47 B4
Shankar	36 A1
Shanti Mukand	34 C2
Sharma	30 B2 35 B3 41 C3 48 A2 52 B2
Sheila	30 B1
Shikla Medicos	34 B2
Shiyam	46 B1
Shroff's Charity Eye	25 D3
Shyam Lal	25 D3
Shyam	46 C1
Singh	30 C1
Sitaram Bharia Institute of Science & Research	38 C2
Sitaram	47 C3
Skin	41 B3
Smt. Girchan Lal Maternity Hospital	24 B3
South Point	41 B4
Spring Meadows	41 C3
St. Stephen's	24 A1
Sucheta Kriplani	20 A1
Sudarshan	52 C1
Sudha	49 B3
Sujan Mahinder	44 B2
Sukhda	41 C4
Sumita	52 C2
Sun Flag	48 B2
Sundar Das Agarwal	52 B2
Surya	34 A1
Swastik	34 C1
Tandon	36 A1
Taneja	34 B2
Tarawati Ramgopal Mehra	35 C3
Tarawati	42 A1
TB Rajan Babu	29 D3
TB	24 A1 44 A2
Temple	25 D3
Tibbia	23 C2
UK	36 A1
Vardaan	41 A4
Vasant Lok	38 B1
Veena	27 C4
Veeran Wali	18 A2
Vet	18 B1 21 C4 24 A1 24 A1 24 A1 29 C3 33 B3 37 A4 39 A3 40 A2
Vimhans	40 C2
Walia	35 A3
Yashoda	47 B3
Yogashram	34 A2

HOTELS & RESTAURANTS

Name	Ref
Agarwal Dharamshala	28 A1 35 A3 48 B1
Agra	25 D3
AIIMS Hostel	40 A2
Airline	24 A3
Ajanta	36 B2
Alcshay Palace	22 B3
Ali's Kathi Kababs	41 B4
Ambassador	21 B4
Anchor Inn	41 C3
Anjalika	22 B3
Ankur Res.	41 A3
Anupam GH	28 A1
Aravali Guest Hostel	38 B2
Aravali Hostel	38 C1
Ashok	18 B2
Ashoka Palace	22 B3
Ashu Villa	44 A1
Asian Intl.	20 A2
Atithi Bhawan	37 B4
Balgopal	25 D3
Basil & Thyme	18 B2
Bavarchi	28 B3
Bhagirath Palace	25 C2
Bharat	24 B2
Blind Students Hostel	29 D3
Brahmaputra Hostel	38 B2
Bright Star Inn	41 C4
Chhabbban Lal Dharamshala	24 A1
Chicken Inn.	21 B3
Chimney's	40 C2
Chopsticks	41 A3
City	24 B3
Claridges	21 A4
Coffee Home	19 A4 35 B3
Cooper Chimney	41 C4
Country Castle	41 C3
Cozy Comer	41 C3
Dakshin	45 A4
Daulat Ram Khan Dharamashala	49 A3
Dawat Khana	44 B2
Dawat	50 A1
Deez	39 B4
Delite	49 A4
Dharamshala	19 C4 31 C3
Dimple	23 C2
Dinar	49 A3
Diplomat	18 B1
Divya	32 B2
Doctor's Hostels	40 A2
Domino's New Delhi Res.	40 A2
Domino's Pizza	22 A3 49 B4 52 A4 44 B2
Dominos	42 B1
Doosri Manzil	52 A4
DPS Hostel	19 A4
Dwarka	41 B4
Eagle	24 B2
El Rancho	44 B2
Ekant	23 D3 48 C1
Farm House	39 C3
First	23 C3
Fish House	39 B4
Fish Point	25 C3
Flora	25 C3
Food Campus	49 B3
Fujiya	18 B1
Ganga Hostel	38 B1
Gaurav	22 B3
Gautam	23 C2
Godavari Hostel	38 B2
Gold Place	23 C3
Grand Hyati	38 A2
Green Channel	48 B2
Groovie	50 C1
Guest House	38 C2
Hans Plaza	20 B1
Hansa Deluxe	22 B3
Highway Inn. GH	28 A1-2
Hill Stone	51 C4
Holiday Home	19 B4
Host Inn.	20 A1
Host	50 C1
Hoste	29 D3l
Hostel	29 D2 48 C1 50 C1
Hyatt Regency	19 B4
ICGB Hostel	38 B2
IIT Hostel	38 C1
Imperial	20 A2
Indraprastha	20 A2
Inter Continental	20 B1
International Inn	40 B2
Intl. Youth Hostel	18 B1
Jain Dharamshala	24 A1
Jaipur Inn	40 B1
Jamia Hostel	44 C2
Janpath	20 A1 20 A2
Jat Dharamshala	37 B4
Jhelum Hostel	38 B1
Jughead's	50 C2
Jukaso	21 C3
Jwalamukhi Hostel	38 C1
Kabear	24 A3
Kabli	401 C1
Kanishka	20 A2
Kapoor Holiday Inn	41 C3
Karakoram Hostel	38 C1
Karim's	21 C4 25 C3
Kastle Guest House	25 D3
Kaveri Hostel	38 B1-2
Kavery	50 C1
Kerala Bhawan	49 A4
Khushal	50 A1
Khyber	24 B1
Kumaon Hostel	38 C1
Kumar	40 C2
Lachman Bagh Hostel	48 B1
Le Meridien	20 A2

Lodhi	21 C4	Women's Hostel	48 B2	YMCA Tourist		20 A1
Madhuban Holiday Inn	41 B3	Regal	24 B1	**MISCELLANEOUS**		
Madina	25 C2	Romana	25 C3	Admn. Block		45 C4
Madras	20 A1	Sabarmati Hostel	38 B1	AJ Farm		39 A4
Maduban	24 A3	Sadhu Palace	24 A3	Ajmere Gate		24 B3
Magpie	48 B2	Sagar	40 B1	All India Boys Scouts Assn.		44 B2
Mahalaxmi Palace	49 A3	Sahara	39 B3	All India Deaf & Dumb Sty.		34 B2
Mahanadi Hostel	38 B2	Samarkand	52 B4	All India Primary Teachers		
Maharaja	24 A1 24 A3 52 A3	Samrat	18 B2 29 D3 47 B4	Federation		37 C3
Maharani	21 C3	Sangam	49 A4	Anu Farm		39 A4
Malika	22 A3	Satkar	49 A4	Arushi's Fun World		50 C1
Manor GH	44 A2	Seth Laxmi Narayan Dharamshala 24 A2		Arya Orphanage		25 C3
Mansarovar Hostel	29 D3	Shafal	24 A3	Ashirwad Farm		39 A4
Marina	20 A1	Shalimar	28 A2	Ashni Farm		39 A4
Mate	50 C1	Shama	50 B2	Assn. of National Brotherhood for		
Maurya Sheraton	18 A2	Shanti Vedna Ashram	19 C4	SocialWelfare		22 B1
Mayur	30 B2 46 A2 49 C4	Sharda	46 A2	Badminton Courts		45 C4
McDonald's	35 B3 41 B3	Sheema	24 B3	Balkunth Farm		39 A4
McDonald's	52 A4	Sheesh Mahal	24 B2	Basket Ball		45 C4
Mela Plaza	46 C2	Shervani Fort View Inn.	21 C3	Bhagri Farm		39 A4
Metro	20 A1 24 B3	Shiela	24 A3	Bhandari Farm		39 A4
Mewa	24 B2	Shipra	47 B3 52 A4	Bhartiya Mahila Jagriti Parishad		38 B1
Milan	49 C3	Shiva	32 AB4	Brahma Kumari Raj Yoga Centre		23 C2
Ming Room	44 B2	Shivalik Hostel	38 C1	Brahma Kumari Spiritual		
Ming Town	28 B2	Shree Balaji	40 B2	Cemetery		36 C2
Mini Moti Mahal	27 B4	Siddharth	22 A3	Chattwal Farm		21 A3
Modern Plaza	47 B3	Silver Oak	41 A4	Chemon Estate		39 A4
Moet's	40 B1	Skylark	46 A2	Chopra Farm		39 A3
Moti Mahal	25 C3 41 B3 48 B2	Skyroom	36 A2	Clock Tower		39 A4
Mughal Mahal	49 A3	Sobti	23 C3	Community Centre		24 B3
Nagaland GH	19 A3	Sodhi Lodge	41 C3	Cremation Ground	25 C1 36 C1 37 A4	38 B1
Narmada Hostel	38 B1	South Indian	22 B3		37 B3 37 B4 42 A2	
Nathu's	44 B2	Southend	18 B1	Cricket		45 C4
Neeru	25 C3	Southern	24 A3	DCW Farm		39 A4
Nest	24 A3	SPA Hostel	44 B1	Delhi Red Cross		21 B4
New Royal	24 B1	SRK Hostel	44 C2	Electric Crematorium		25 D2
Nilgiri Hostel	38 C1	Star	24 A2	Elence Farm		39 A4
Nirula's	19 B3 20 A1 35 B3 38 B1	Sun Village	40 B2	Escorts Rehabilitation Centre		45 B3
	39 A3 39 B3 40 B1 41 C3 22 B3	Surya	40 C2	Federation of Assn.of		
Nurses Hostels	19 C4	Taj Mahal	21 A3	Small Inds. of India		22 B1
Oberoi	21 C4	Taj Palace	18 A2	Foot Ball		
Orchid	40 A2	Taj	25 C3	Gupta Farm		39 A4
Park Royal	41 C3	Teachers Hostel	44 C2	Harcharan Farm		39 B4
Park View	24 B2	Tera	24 B1	ICRC		21 B4
Park	20 A1	Top Food	27 B4	Indira Gandhi Sports Complex		20 C1
Pavitra	36 C2	Tourist	24 A3 40 C1	Instituion of valuers		22 A1
Payal	24 A3	Travel Lodge	24 B1	Institutional Plots		45 C4
Pelican	46 A2	Udupi	38 B1	International Trade Tower		41 C3
Periyar Hostel	38 B1	Upkar Guest Hse.	44 B2	Jahanpanah City Forest		41 B4
PG Girls Hostel	42 B2	Vaishnaw	24 B2	Jahaz Farm		39 A4
Phoolwari	20 C2	Vasant Continental	38 B1	Jain Mahila Ashram		25 D3
Pizza Corner	41 B3	Vig	25 C2	Jasola Sports Complex		45 C4
Pizza Hut	41 B3 52 A4	Vikram	40 B2	Jawaharlal Nehru Memorial Fund		18 C1
Plaza Solitaire	50 C1	Vikrant	24 B1 29 D3	Kalasho Farm		39 A4
Punjab	24 B2	Vivek	24 A3	Kashmere Gate		24 B1
Qutb	38 C2	West Bengal Guest House	18 B1	Khurana Farm		39 A4
Rail Yatri Niwas	24 B3	Wheels	50 B1	Kochnar Farm		39 A4
Raj Mahal Deluxe	50 B1	Wimpy	35 B3 40 C2 41 B3 49 B3 52 A4	Lawn Tennis Courts		45 C4
Rajendra	22 A3	Windsor Place	41 A4	Leprosy Society		40 C2
Rang Mahal	24 A1	Working Womens		Ma Anandmayee Ashram		45 B4
Ranjit	20 B1	Hostel	38 C2 44 C2 50 B2	Manchanda Farm		39 A4
Red Cross Working		YMCA Guest Hse.	20 A2	Mani Prabha Farm		39 A3

Mata Amritanadmayi Math	39 A4
Maulana Azad's Tomb	25 C2
Mehta Farm	39 A4
Nature Cure & Yoga Centre	45 A3
North Gate	38 B1
Okhla Compost Plant	45 B3
Open Scrub	37 B4
Parliamentarian Language Samiti	18 C1
Poultry Farm	39 A4 39 C4
Rai Farm	39 A4
Ram Krishna Sevashram	44 A2
Razia Begum'sTomb	25 BC3
Red Cross Sty.	48 C2
Regional Testing Lab	45 A3
Rohini Sports Complex	27 C3
Rohtash Farm	39 A4
RoseGarden Farm	39 A4
Russian Trade Federation	18 A2
Sabvana Farm	39 A4
Sahara Satya Ashram	49 B4
Sahgal Farm	39 A4
Sant Asa Ram Bapu Ashram	23 C3
Sant Nirankari Ashram	30 B2
Satkar Farm	39 A4
Shakti Punj Farm	39 A4
Skating Rink	45 C4
Sports Complex	40 A1
Squash Courts	45 C4
Student Activity Centre	38 B1
Sunrise Farm	39 A4
Surat Villa Farm	39 A4
Syal Farm	39 A4
Thapar Farm	39 A4
Theosophical Society	22 A3
Tibetan SOS Youth Hostel	27 C3
Town Hall	25 B2
Transit House	38 B2
Turkman Gate	25 C3
Volley Ball	45 C4
Yamuna Velodrome	20 C1

MUSEUMS & ART GALLERIES

Ahinsa Sthal	39 C3
AIFACS.	20 A2
Archaeological Museum	25 D2
Art Today	20 A1
Bapu Bapa	29 D2
Crafts Museum	21 C3
Dolls Museum	20 C1
Dr. Zakir Husain Memorial Museum	44 C2
Field Museum	21 C3
Gallery	40 B2
Gallery Espace	44 B2
Gallery Ganesha	41 C4
Garhi Studio	40 C2
Indian Art Corner	21 C4
Indian War Memorial Museum	25 C2
Indira Gandhi Memorial	18 C2
Indira Gandhi National Centre for Arts	20 A2
Jawaharlal Nehru Memorial Museum	18 C1
Ladakh	21 C3
Mansur	40 C2
National Children's Museum	20 B1
National Gallery of Modern Art	21 B3
National Museum	20 B1 21 A3
National Police Museum	21 B4
National Rail Museum	19 A3
National Science Centre	21 C3
Nehru Planetarium	18 B1
Nigam Rangshala	25 B2
Regional Museum	50 C2
Srinivasa Mallah Theatre Crafts Museum	20 B1
Sulabh Museum of Toilets	37 A4
Swatantrata Sangram Sangrahalaya	25 C2
Tibet Hse.	21 B4
Vadera	40 B2

PLACES OF WORSHIP
TEMPLES

Aparna Ashram	44 A2
Arya Samaj Mandir	41 B3 41 C4
Baha'i House of Worship	45 A3
Balmiki Mandir	27 A4
Banke Bihari	48 A2
Bhairon	18 B2 21 C3
Bhairon	45 A3
Dada Bari	40 A2
Devi	21 C3
Diviya Mandir	29 C3
Dudhia Bhairon	21 C3
Durga Bari Mandir	41 C3
Durga	45 A3
Gauri Shankar	25 C2
Geeta Mandir	48 B1 49 B3
Hanuman Mandir	25 C1
Hanuman Setu	25 C1
Hanuman	20 A1
ISKCON	45 A3
Jain Mandir	25 C2 39 C4 48 C2
Jain	20 A1
Jat Fauji Dharamshala	25 C1
Jogmaya Mandir	39 C3
Kailash Shiv Mandir	45 A3
Kali Mandir	41 C4
Kalkaji Mandir	45 A3
Laxmi Narayan	48 B2
Lotus Temple	45 A3
Mahavir Mandir	41 B3
Malcha	18 B1
Mata Mandir	23 D3
Nigambodh Ghat	25 C1
Parsi Fire Temple	20 C1
Ram Mandir	39 A4
Saraswati Vidya Mandir	46 B1
Satya Narayan Mandir	42 A2
Sehja Yoga Mandir	38 C2
Shakti Peeth	39 C3
Sheetla	40 C2
Shiv Mandir	43 B3
Shri Ram Dharamshala	39 C3-4
Venkateshwara	38 C1

GURUDWARA

Bala Sahib	44 A1
Mata Sundari	20 B1

CHURCHES

Akshya Pratishthan	39 A4
Holiy Trinity	25 C3
Isha Bhavana	45 B3
St.James' Church	24 B1
St.Stephen's	24 B2

MOSQUES

Afsar Wala Masjid	21 C4
Allaudin's Tomb	39 C3
Ashiq Allah	39 B3
Auliya Masjid	39 C4
Bakibillah Shah's	24 A2
Balban's Tomb	39 C3
Bhul Bhulaiyan	39 C3
Dargah Chiragh Dehivi	41 B4
Dargah Mamoo Bhanja	23 D2
Dargah Qutbuddin Bakhtiyar Kaki	39 C3
Dargah Sharif	32 A2
Dargah	39 C3
Fakr-ul Masajid	24 B1
Fatehpuri Masjid	24 B2
Ghata Masjid	25 D3
Haj Manzil	25 C3
Hauz i Shamsi	39 B4
Hazrat Nizamuddin Aulia Dargah	21 C4
Imarn Zamin's Tomb	39 C3
Indraprastha Bwn.	20 C1
Jahaz Mahal	39 C4
Jama Masjid	25 C2
Jamali Kamali	39 C3-4
Jharna	39 C4
Jinnabadi	39 C4
Kadam Shariff	24 A3
Kalan Masjid	24 B3
Kale Khan	20 B1
Karbala	40 A1
Lal Gumbad	41 A4
Lal Mahal	39 C4
Madhi Masjid	39 C4
Maqdum Shah Masjid	39 B4
Masjid Chakarwali	21 C4
Masjid Idgah	51 B3
Matka Peer	20 C2
Moth ki Masjid	40 A2
Mubarak Shah's Tomb	40 A1
Mughal Kos Minar	45 C4
Najafkhan's Tomb	40 A1
Nazaria Pir Ashiq Allah	39 B4
New Sabzi Mandi	31 C4
Pahari Wali Masjid	39 C4
Pare Wali Masjid	39 C4
Parisilla Bwn.	20 C2
Qila kuhna Masjid	21 C3
Quwwaful Islam Masjid	39 C3
Rang Mahal	39 C4
Shahi Idgah	23 D2 39 B3
Sikandar Lodi's Tomb	21 A4

Sohan Burj	39 C4	Ganga Cplx.	52 B4		36 B1 37 C3 45 A3 52 B3
Sunehri Masjid	25 C2	Godavari Cplx.	52 B4	The Presidency	50 C1
Sunehri	24 BC2	Gokhale Mkt.	24 A1	Transport Market	49 A4
Tahwar Khan	24 A2	Govinda Cplx.	50 C1	Triveni Shopping Centre	41 A4
Vikas Bwn.	20 C2	Gurjar Market	36 C1	Vishal Mkt.	29 D2
Zafar Mahal	39 C3	Guru Nanak Market	50 A1	Yusuf Zai Mkt.	20 A1
		Harvansh Singh Mkt.	42 A2		
RAILWAY STATIONS		Hint House	46 B2	**TRAVEL AGENCIES**	
AzadpurRS.	28 A3	Huda Shopping Cplx.	50 A1	Destination Travels	19 B3
Dayabasti RS.	22 A1	INA Mkt.	19 C4	Jyoti Travels	50 A1
Delhi Main RS.	24 B1	Islam Nagar Market	46 A2	Travel Spirits Intl.	21 B3
Faridabad New Town RS.	49 A4	Jaina Tower	46 B2	United World Travels	41 B3
Faridabad RS.	48 A1	Kallupura Mkt.	47 B3		
Kishan Ganj RS.	23 C1	Kamla Mkt.	24 B3	**WEDDING HALLS**	
LajpatNgr. RS.	40 C1	Kamps Plaza	27 B4	Amber	36 B1
Lodi Colony RS.	40 A1	Kanishka Shopping Plaza	20 A2	Ashirwad	34 A1 36 A2
New Delhi RS.	24 A3	Kashmir Govt. Arts Emporium	21 A4	Atithi	29 C2
Okhla RS.	45 A3	Kendriya Bhandar	52 C4	Bawa Palace	35 A3
Pragati Maidan RS.	20 C2	Khan Mkt.	21 B4	Chandan Chetan	44 A1
Sabzi Mandi RS.	23 C1	Khanna Mkt.	24 A1	City Palace	34 A1
Sadar Bazar RS.	24 A2	Krit Plaza	34 C1	Delhi Darbar	28 A3
Sahibabad RS.	32 C2	Lajpat Rai Mkt.	25 C2	Dolphin	29 C3
Sarai Rohilla RS.	22 B1	Lakshmi Bazar	50 A2	Dwarka	36 B1
Sewa Ngr. RS.	40 B1	Lamba Enterprises	36 C1	Ganga	32 B1
Shahdara RS.	31 C4	Laxmi Mkt. East	34 A2	Gola	28 B3
Shivaji Bridge RS.	20 B1	Laxmi Mkt. West	34 A2	Jhankar	34 B2
Tilak Bridge RS.	20 BC2	Leela Ram Market	40 A2	Kashish	35 B3
Vivekanand Puri Rs.	22 B1	Marble Market	49 B3	Lagan	35 B3
		Meena Bazar	25 C2 25 C2	Lajwab	34 B2
SHOPPING CENTRES		Mehar Chand Market	40 B1	Laxmi Palace	48 B1
Ambedkar Rd. Mkt.	47 B3	Munirka Market	38 B1	Laxmi	30 B2
Amrit Kaur Mkt.	24 A3	Nagar Palika.	47 A3	Maharaja	36 A2
Anaj Mandi	23 D1	Narain Mkt.	24 A2	Marriage Home	46 B1
Anguribagh Mkt.	25 C1	Navyug Market	46 A2	Marriage Point	49 A4
Ansal Plaza	40 A2	New Rashid Mkt.	34 A2	Mehfil	28 B3
Archana Shopping Centre	41 B3	Okhla Sabzi Mandi	45 A3	Milan Hall	35 A3
Ashish	34 B2	Om Mkt.	52 C2	New Madhur Milan	41 B3
Atta Mkt.	52 A4	Pal Mohan Plaza	23 C2	Oak Wood	37 A4
Azad Mkt.	24 A1	Palika Bazar	20 A1 50 A1	Panchshila Rendezvous	41 A4
Balaji Plaza	27 C4 28 B3	Palika Mkt.	19 B4	Pooja	31 C3
Balbir Mkt.	47 B3 47 B3	Pooja Mkt.	52 C1	Raunaqe	34 A1
Balupura Mkt.	47 B3	Pragati Mkt.	28 A3	Right Choice	35 B3
Begum Zaidi Mkt.	19 A3	Prithiviraj Mkt.	21 B4	Ronald Palace	49 A3
Bhagat Singh Mkt.	47 B3	Pushpa Tower	47 B3	Royal Court	40 C2
Brahmaputra Shopping Cplx.	52 B4	Rajendra Mkt.	24 A1	Ruby	47 B4
Central Market	36 C1 40 C2	Rashid Mkt.	34 A2	Sahara	39 B3-4
Chandi Plaza	41 C3	Rui Mkt.	24 A1	Sanvaria	49 B4
Chandrapuri Market	46 A2	Sabzi Mandi	31 B4	Shabnam	42 B1
Chhotti Sabzi Mandi	36 B1	Sagar	34 B2	Shri Ram	30 B2
Cloth Mkt.	24 B1	Santushti Shopping Arcade	18 C2	Shubham	30 A2
Commercial Cplx.	51 C3	Satyam	46 B2	Suhaag	36 C1
Computer Cplx.	45 C4	Savitri Complex	47 B4	Surat Gardens	39 A4
Damodar Cplx.	52 B4	Savitri Mkt.	52 A4	Swagat	36 B1
Dasna Gate Mkt.	47 A3	Shakti Mkt.	52 A4	Tara	40 C2
Dayal Market	46 A2	Shankar Mkt.v	20 A1	Umang	36 B1
DDA Shopping Complex	41 B3	Shastri Mkt.	28 A2	Vatika	20 C2
Delhi Gate Mkt.	47 A3	Shivaji Mkt.	27 C4	Vividha	35 B3
Dilli Haat	19 C4	Shubham Plaza	48 B1	Wayamvar	32 C1
Durga Chamber	46 B2	Special Market	49 B3		
Flower Market	39 C3	Subhash Market	40 B1		
Gaffar Market	22 B3	Subzi Mandi	50 B2		
Gandhi Mkt.	24 B2	Suchita Complex	47 B3		
Gandhi Nagar Mkt.	47 B3	Super Bazar	19 C4 20 A1 20 B2		

(Continuation from page 16)

Qudsia Garden

This garden, on the banks of the Yamuna, was laid out in 1748 by Qudsia Begum, a slave girl who later became Muhammed Shah's favourite mistress. Also associated with the historical mutiny of 1857, the garden now contains a wide variety of flowers and an imposing gateway, where peacocks can be found in abundance.

Roshanara Bagh

This popular garden is a favourite retreat for the residents of crowded old Delhi. Laid out in 1650, by Roshanara Begum, Shahjahan's daughter, the garden contains a variety of roses, a Japanese garden and a network of water channels.

Talkatora Garden

This bowl-shaped garden complex at Willingdon Crescent, with mini lakes and fountains, attracts picnickers throughout the year. The swimming complex and modern stadium are the venue of many national and international sporting events.

MONUMENTS AND MEMORIALS

Chandni Chouk

Once the pulse of Mughal Delhi's commercial life, Chandni Chouk is today, the centrepiece of old Delhi. Designed by Jahanara Begum, the favourite daughter of Shah Jahan in 1648, this place was once filled with shops and houses of wealthy merchants and noblemen. A narrow watercourse once flowed down the middle of this road, carrying water to the palaces. Its winding narrow lanes are now filled with a variety of shops ranging from sweet stalls to jewellery, textile and leather shops.

Ferozshah Kotla

The site of the city of Ferozabad built in the 14th century by Emperor Ferozshah Tughlaq. The famous 14-metre high polished sandstone Ashoka pillar can be found here.

Humayun's Tomb

A synthesis of the Persian and Indian building styles, this magnificent memorial was built by Haji Begum, Humayun's senior widow. The tomb complex is a harmonious blend of architecture and nature, as the mausoleum is surrounded by avenues of trees, watercourses and flowerbeds. Built with red sandstone and marble, the mausoleum also contains the tombs of many other members of the Mughal dynasty.

India Gate

A memorial to the unknown soldier, India Gate was initially designed by Lutyens, as the All India War Memorial arch, in honour of the 90,000 Indian soldiers who lost their lives in World War I. This 42 metre high structure has the names of soldiers engraved all over it. An eternal flame burns here, in commemoration of the Unknown Soldier. Located at the East End of Rajpath, India Gate provides a spectacular view of the Rashtrapati Bhavan and its surrounding lawns. Sunset at India Gate, when the arch and the fountains are illuminated with colourful lights, is truly an exhilarating experience.

Indira Gandhi Memorial

No. 1 Safdarjung Road, the house where Indira Gandhi lived and died, is a striking contrast when compared to Teen Murthi House, her father's Mansion. The modestly furnished rooms and the books, letters, photographs and paintings on display provide a fascinating insight into the private life of Indira Gandhi. The speeches of Mrs. Gandhi played through speakers hidden in the bushes, and the bloodstain on the pathway, are a solemn reminder of this charismatic leader.

Jama masjid

The mosque, the largest in India, was built by Shah Jahan in 1658 A.D. Situated near the Red Fort in old Delhi, the Jama Masjid has a seating capacity of more than 20,000. Crowned by three onion domes and tapering minarets made of marble and slate, this architectural beauty is also a place of religious significance. There is a marble tank in the middle of the mosque, where devotees wash before attending prayers. The view from the top of the minarets is excellent. A visit to Jama Masjid is never complete without visiting the neighbouring streets, which are important commercial shopping centres. The Muslim restaurants here provide excellent *tandoori* and *Mughlai* food.

Jantar Mantar

Maharaja Jai Singh's observatory Jantar Mantar, is located near the junction of Parliament street and Connaught Circus. Built with the main objective of standardizing almanacs, the place is filled with huge concrete astronomical 'instruments' which were used to plot the course of heavenly bodies, and predict eclipses. Notable among these structures is a huge sundial, popularly known as "the prince of sun dials".

The National Samadhis

Along the banks of the Yamuna, near Raj Ghat, are **Shanti Vana** – the place where Nehru was cremated, and **Vijay Ghat**, the samadhi of Lal Bahadur Shastri. Closeby are the Samadhis of Indira Gandhi – **Shakti Sthal**, and her sons Sanjay and Rajiv Gandhi.

Tughlakabad

The ruins of Tughlakabad, the third city of Delhi, are located on rocky landscape, about 10 km east of Qutab complex, along the Mahrauli Badarpur road. The fort here contains bastioned ramparts, underground chambers, tall gateways and towers which lend the place an air of solemn grandeur. Notable among the buildings here is **Ghiyas-ud-din's Mausoleum** built of marble and red sandstone. At the southeast corner of Tughlakabad, is the **Adilabad Fort**.

Purana Qila

Purana Qila, the sixth city of Delhi, is today the most important monument in Delhi. Located southeast of India gate, near Nizamuddin Railway station, Purana Qila was originally the city of Indraprastha, the legendary site of the epic Mahabharatha. The massive gateways and walls of Purana Qila were initially built by Humayun who called the citadel Dinpanah. The Qila-i-Kuhna Masjid, Sher Mandal, Khairu'l Mazil Masjid and other buildings found here were built by Sher Shah, who defeated Humayun and renamed the city Sher Garh. The archaeological findings unearthed here are on display at the field museum. Purana Qila presents a truly majestic sight, when floodlit, with splendid gateways and pavilions etched against the night sky. An imposing view of Purana Qila can be had from the neighbouring zoological gardens also.

A spectacular Sound and Light Show depicting scenes from Delhi's historic and legendary past is held here on Tuesdays, Thursdays, Saturdays and Sundays.

Qutab Minar Complex

One of Delhi's most striking monuments is the 278 feet high **Qutab Minar**, which

Qutab Minar

Red Fort

looms majestically across the wide plains of Delhi. Started by Qutb-ud-din Aibak and completed by Firoz Shah Tughlak in 1368 AD, the tower contains many ornamental inscriptions and four projecting balconies. Built initially as a tower of victory, it was also used by the muezzin to call the faithful to prayer.

Among the ruins in the Qutab Complex, the **Quwat ul Islam Masjid** is one of the most magnificent mosques in the world. The building material for this mosque was provided by demolishing many Hindu and Jain temples in this area. Built in 1197, this mosque is one of the finest blends of Hindu and Islamic architecture.

In the courtyard of the Quwat-ul-Islam Mosque, is a seven metre high **Iron Pillar** – one of Delhi's most curious antiquities. Belonging to the Gupta age, the pillar contains Sanskrit inscriptions that state its history. Made of 98% wrought iron, the pillar speaks for the metallurgical skill of ancient India, as it has withstood several centuries without rusting. According to popular folklore, a person who can encircle the pillar with his arms behind will have his wishes granted. Few leave the place without trying.

Raj Ghat

This serene spot on the west bank of river Yamuna is where the mortal remains of Mahatma Gandhi were cremated. The samadhi is surrounded by wide lawns and a garden with fountains and exotic trees.

Directly opposite Raj Ghat is the **Gandhi Memorial Museum**, where photographs, manuscripts and other personal belongings of Gandhiji are on display. The museum also has an amphitheater and library.

Lal Qila (Red Fort)

The very epitome of Mughal grandeur, the Red fort now forms a part and parcel of Indian history. Built out of red sandstone, this massive fort and palace were constructed by Shahjahan in 1648. The Red fort is today, a calm haven amidst the busy streets of old Delhi. In its ruins can be seen the power and elegance of the Mughal empire.

The main entrance to the fort is the **Lahori Gate**. Flanked by towers and a central archway this place was once a royal market where jewellers, painters and specialised craftsmen lived and sold their wares. The National flag of independent India was unfurled by Jawaharlal Nehru on 15th August 1947, in the ramparts of this gate. This event is repeated every year. This arcade leads into the double-storeyed **Naubat Khana**, which was once the musician's gallery.

Diwan-i-Am, the hall of public audience, was the place where the emperor held court and met dignitaries and foreign emissaries. The most fascinating feature here is the alcove in the back wall filled with the fine examples of Italian *pietra-dura* work.

The most magnificent and exclusive of all buildings here, is the **Diwan-i-Khas**, the hall of private audience. This pavilion of white marble, supported by intricately carved pillars, is richly decorated with inlaid mosaic work. This hall once contained the famous peacock throne, which was later plundered by Nadir Shah.

The **Hamams** or royal baths can be found near the Diwan-i-khas. Bathing being a favourite past time of the Mughals, these luxurious apartments contained rose-scented fountains, steam and hot water baths and dressing rooms.

Once the residence of the senior queens, the **Rang Mahal** (hall of colours) has private rooms with intricately carved screens. In the middle of the hall is a lotus-shaped ivory fountain, which once formed a part of the Stream of Paradise that flowed through the main hall.

Pragati Maidan

Diwan-i-Am

Other important buildings inside Red Fort are, the Khas Mahal, Moti Mahal, Musammam Burg and Chatta Chowk. The **Red Fort Museum** has on display, armoury, textiles, jewellery and manuscripts belonging to the Mughal era.

History repeats itself in these gardens and palaces, as the **Sound and Light Spectacle** recreates the dramatic events associated with the fort. Hindi and English shows are held daily in the evenings.

Safdarjung's tomb

One of the last examples of Mughal architecture, Safdarjung's tomb stands in the centre of an extensive garden. Build in 1753 by Safdarjung's son the tomb has various chambers and spacious pavilions with ornamental ceilings and polygonal towers inlaid with marble. A bulbous marble dome can be found in the centre of this mausoleum.

MUSEUMS AND ART GALLERIES

Air Force Museum

This museum near Palam has on display, aircrafts, bullets, guns, uniforms and photographs, tracing the history of the Indian Air Force. Drop in while waiting for a delayed flight, it's the perfect place to spend your time.

Closed on Mondays, Tuesdays and National Holidays.

Crafts Museum

Located at Bhairon Road in Pragathi Maidan, this museum showcases a variety of crafts from different parts of India. Regular demonstrations are held by craftsmen and a small crafts shop is also located here.

Doll's Museum

Started by the Cartoonist Shankar in 1954, as a personal collection, the museum has today, more than 6000 dolls from all over the world. Located on Bahadur Shah Zafar Marg, the museum campus also has a doll-designing centre and Children's Library within its premises. Closed on Mondays.

Gandhi Smriti Museum

Located in Tees January Marg, this museum has an interesting collection of memorabilia on Gandhiji. There is an exhibition of dolls depicting important milestones in Gandhiji's life. Khadi and village industry products are also sold here.

National Gallery of Modern Art

The former residential palace of the Maharaja of Jaipur now houses an excellent collection of over 3,700 paintings, graphics and sculpture belonging to the school of modern art. Notable among the works on display, are the paintings and sculptures of Daniells, E.B. Havell, Jamini Roy, Amrita Shergill and Rabindranath Tagore. Special exhibitions are arranged periodically, to display works from private collections and foreign museums. Researchers and students can make use of the library, which contains information about contemporary art.

Timings: 10.00 am to 5.00 pm. Closed on Mondays and Holidays.

National Museum

Located at the junction of Janpath and Rajpath, the National Museum displays a rich collection of the artistic treasures of India and Central Asia. Established in 1950, the museum is enriched by selective exhibits from state Museums and private collections. Special sections have been devoted for pre-historic displays, medieval art pieces, manuscripts and miniature paintings. The collection of Indian costumes, silver work and Indian musical instruments are some of the main attractions here. An excellent library and daily film shows provide further information. Replicas of articles on display are sold at the entrance.

Timings: 10.00 am to 5.00 pm. Closed on Mondays.

National Museum of Natural History

Located on Barakhamba Road, this museum has various galleries that throw light on ecology and the earth's natural resources. Children can play and learn in the activity rooms here.

Rail Transport Museum

The Rail Museum has on display, 26 vintage locomotives, 17 quaint carriages and saloons and many interesting exhibits, which trace the 140-year-old history of the Indian Railways. Located on a ten-acre site near the Diplomatic

Gandhi Smriti Museum

Enclave, this Museum established in 1977, is the first of its kind in India. Among the prize exhibits are the "Fairie Queen" (1855) – the oldest working stream locomotive still in excellent condition, a tiny Darjeeling Himalayan Railway engine and the luxurious saloon used by the Prince of Wales in 1876. But don't miss the Mysore Maharaja's saloon – made of seasoned teak and laced with gold and Ivory.

Natioanl Museum

Timings:
April-September : 09.30 am to 19.30 pm
October-March : 09.30 am to 17.30 pm
Closed on Mondays

Red Fort Museum of Archaeology

A splendid collection of curios and artifacts from the Mughal period, including a manuscript copy of the Holy Koran in Nasq characters, are on display here.

Red Fort Museum of Arms & Weapons

This museum illustrates the chronological development of arms and armour from the Mughal period till the First World War.

Teen Murti Bhavan (Nehru Museum)

Built as a part of imperial Delhi, the Teen Murti Bhavan became the official residence of Jawaharlal Nehru, when he assumed office as the first Prime Minister of independent India. The house was converted into a museum after his death in 1964. The garden, library, lawn and the mementos and pictures on display are a vivid reminder of Nehru's multi-faceted personality.

The furnishing, desk, library and bedroom in his private quarters are being maintained as he left them. A sound and light show is held here everyday after sunset.

Tibet House Museum

Located on Lodi Road, this museum depicts the richness of Tibetan culture and art. The collection includes *thankas*, old currency notes, head pieces, prayer objects and musical instruments besides a library and emporium.

EXCURSIONS

Agra *(203 km)*
The city of the Taj, contains many interesting monuments – including the world famous **Taj Mahal**. Located on the west bank of the Yamuna, this white marble monument is truly a sight to behold on a moonlit night. The other places of interest here, are the Agra Fort, Sikandra and the deserted city of Fatehpur Sikri.

Ballabgarh Lake *(36km)*
Located on the Delhi-Mathura road, this tourist resort is ideal for a quiet holiday. Fishing in the lake can be both exciting and rewarding.

Bhalswa Lake
The multi-sport and leisure complex set up by Delhi Tourism offers facilities for boating, kayaking, canoeing and angling.

Corbett National Park *(263 km)*
Named after the famous hunter-naturalist Jim Corbett, the park is located on the undulating foothills of the Himalayas. Spread over 520 sq. kms. of grasslands and thick forests, with the Ramganga river flowing through it, the park contains a variety of wild animals including tiger, elephant, leopard, mugger crocodile and gharial.

Season: February to May.

Taj Mahal

Debchick *(92 km)*

Set amidst well-landscaped surroundings, this tourist complex on Agra highway, is known for its entertainment activities which include camel and elephant rides, folk dancers and snake charmers.

Jaipur *(258 km)*

The capital of Rajasthan, Jaipur is popularly known as the "Pink city", because of the stone used in its buildings. It is the home of the colourful warrior Rajputs, whose rich attire makes up for the drab desert landscape. The Amber fort and the Hawa Mahal with its latticed windows are worth seeing.

Keoladeo Ghana National Park *(215 km)*

This bird sanctuary of Bharatpur, is one of the greatest and most important heronries in the world. Made up of shallow, fresh-water marshes, thorn, scrub and mixed deciduous forests, the park has an annual migrant population of over 5,00,000 birds. Nearly 100 species of birds, including the Siberian crane and a variety of ducks visit the park every year for breeding.

Season: August to February.

Sariska Tiger Reserve *(239 km)*

This tiger reserve is made up of dry deciduous forests, which form a part of the Aravalli range of mountains. A wide variety of animals including tiger, sambar and wild boar can be seen here at the water holes. The park also contains 9th century ruins of Shiva temples and the Kanokwari fort.

Season: November to June.

Sohna *(58 km)*

Located around the Sohna fort, the hot sulphur springs here are said to have medicinal properties. This tourist complex has excellent facilities for board and lodging.

Sultanpur Bird Sanctuary *(46 km)*

This large lake near Gurgaon, attracts a large number of resident and migratory birds from Europe, Siberia and Central Asia. The sanctuary is exceptionally beautiful in winter when grey saurus cranes and long-legged white flamingoes visit this place.

Surajkund *(17 km)*

This picnic spot near Delhi is the site of a famous temple and an amphitheater in ruins. The modern tourist facilities at Surajkund Lake include an 18-hole golf course, boating and fishing facilities.

EATING OUT

Delhiites are connoisseurs of good food. The choice of eating places are wide and varied and sometimes, bewildering. One can dine at elegant restaurants in five-star surroundings, but there are also several smaller places that serve delectable fare.

Fast food joints are the in-places now. But nothing can match the thrill of eating spicy chaat dished up by roadside vendors. Chaat is a delicious potpourri of a snack that comes in a variety of recipes – as gol gappas, papri, alu ki chaat and kulla, to name just a few.

Gol gappas are also known as paani puris. Small hollow balls made of wheat flour are fried in oil and filled with jeera-pani (sweetened cumin water), spiced with red and black pepper. What results is the most popular kind of chaat.

Papris are flat gol gappas dipped in curd and arranged on a plate with potatoes and channa (gram) spiced with peppers, chillies and sonth (a thick sauce made from tamarind and coriander).

Aloo ki chaat is a preparation of roasted potatoes seasoned with hot spices, jeera-paani and lime juice.

Kulla, another potato-preparation, is a roasted potato stuffed with chick peas, lime juice, hot spices and red pepper.

More than anything else, however, Delhi's speciality is Mughlai and Tandoor food.

Mughlai food is the result of a distinctive style of cooking which reached its zenith in the days of the later Mughal kings, though it originated during the times of the Turks and Afghans who ruled Delhi some 400 years before the Mughals.

Mughlai cuisine, which is based on the original recipes of Mughal emperors, is marked by a richness that one naturally associates with the grandiose, leisurely Mughal life-style. Meat and chicken dishes marinated in yoghurt and spices and flavoured with fragrant saffron are Mughlai specialities. Biryani - an exotic dish of flavoured rice and meat, is the staple of every Mughlai feast. Succulent Kababs (grilled meat preparations) are another delicacy. While the bigger restaurants serve good Mughlai food, the most authentic fare can be savoured in the small restaurants in the Jama Masjid area.

Many of today's tastiest Mughal dishes are mentioned in Ain-e-Akbari – Akbar's Regulations – written by the emperor's court historian and close friend, Abul Fazl. Perusing this book is certainly worth the time spent for any one on the lookout for original recipes.

Tandoori cuisine gets its name from tandoor – an underground clay oven with a low temperature over which the tandoor specialities – marinated chicken, meat, fish and prawns and a variety of breads – are slowly grilled. Tandoori cooking, which is very much like Middle Eastern cuisine, has its origins in the north-west frontier of the sub-continent. Varieties of tandoori breads are also common accompaniments to Mughlai meat dises.

Delhi offers a wide selection of restaurants to choose from, each unique in its own way. Some of the recommended ones are:

RESTAURANTS

Indian

Blues
N-18, Outer Circle, Connaught Place, Delhi Phone: 47078888, 9810120995
Timings: 12:00 pm to midnight (Happy Hours: 4.00 p.m. - 8.00 p.m.)

Colonel's Kebabz
29, Defence Colony Market, Defence Colony, Delhi Phone: 24338137, 24330136
Timings: 11:00 am to 12:00 pm

Chaska
PU-8, Near Ramlila Ground, Pitampura, Delhi Phone: 27346081, 27346181, 65106081 Timings: 11:00 am to 11:00 pm

Dwarka
3F, Kamla Nagar, Delhi
Phone: 23840078, 23845234,
Timings: 8:00 am to 11:00 pm

Evergreen
5-29-30, Ground & First Floor, Green Park, Delhi Phone: 26514646, 26856774,
Timings: 9:00 am to 10:30 pm

Flaming Mustard
1249, Aruna Asaf Ali Marg, Near D-3 Crossing, Vasant Vihar, Delhi
Phone: 30994625, 9810210275
Timings: 11:00 am to 11:00 pm

Jade Garden
5/66, Padam Singh Road, WEA, Karol Bagh, Delhi Phone: 25747555, 41450283
Timings: 11:00 am to midnight

Moti Mahal
M 30, Market, Greater Kailash I, Delhi
Phone: 26412467, 26280480
Timings: 12:00 pm to 3:30 pm, 7:00 pm to 12:00 pm

Pind Baluchi
J-2/1, B K Dutta Market, Rajouri Garden, Delhi Phone: 64172511, 25421725,
Timings: 12:00 pm to 3:15 pm, 6:30 pm to 11:15 pm

Rajinder Da Dhaba
AB-14, Opposite Safdarjung Club, DDA Market, Safdarjung Enclave, Delhi
Phone: 41650542, 9868720969
Timings: 5:00 pm to 11:00 pm

Ramas Cafe
6/79, Padam Singh Road, Karol Bagh, Delhi
Phone: 25760785
Timings: 7:00 am to 11:00 pm

Saravana Bhavan
46, Janpath, Connaught Place, Delhi
Phone: 23317755, 23316060
Timings: 8:00 am to 11:00 pm

Sahni Bhojan Bhandar
2157/B2, Guru Arjun Nagar, Opp. West Patel Nagar, Near Shadipur Metro Station, Patel Nagar, Delhi, Phone: 25709987, 9873786020
Timings: 10:00 am to 4:00 am

Shaan-E-Dill
1148, Behind Scindia House, Connaught Place, Delhi
Phone: 23316578
Timings: 11:00 am to 10:45 pm

Sampoorna Dakshin
F20, Distt. Centre, Janakpuri, Delhi
Phone: 25559999, 25537777, 25557777
Timings: 11:00 am to 11:00 pm

Sanskriti
F-8, Janak Place, District Centre, Janakpuri, Delhi
Phone: 25526325, 41589736
Timings: 11:00 am to 11:00 pm

Udupi's Dosa Corner
72, Khanna Market, Lodhi Colony, Lodhi Road, Delhi. Phone: 24647872, 9811107287
Timings: 8:30 am to 11:00 pm

Volga
18-B, Connaught Place, Delhi
Phone: 23322960 Timings: 1:00 pm to 4:00 pm, 6:00 pm to 11:00 pm

Wok in the Clouds
J-2I13, Rajouri Garden, Delhi
Ph: 25922097, 25922098, 25922099
Timings: 11:00 am to 11:45 pm

Zaika
C9/25, Sector 7, Rohini, Delhi
Phone: 27295693, 27883310
Timings: 10:00 am to 11:00 pm

Chinese

China Town
The Ashok, 50 B, Chanakyapuri, Delhi
Phone: 26110101, 26873216, 26878887, 26878885, 26878862
Timings: 12:30 pm to 2:45 pm, 7:30 pm to 11:30 pm

China Bowl
11, Satya Niketan Market, Dhaula Kuan, Delhi Phone: 26111724
Timings: 11:00 am to 11:00 pm

Lazeez
2, New Rajdhani Enclave, Opposite Taneja Hospital, Vikas Marg, Preet Vihar, Delhi
Phone: 22046666, 42441112
Timings: 11:00 am to 11:00 pm

Moet's
50, Defence Colony Market, Defence Colony, Delhi Phone: 41550571
Timings: 12:00 pm to midnight

Pik Wik
66, Shakti Vihar, Pitampura, Delhi
Phone: 27016192, 27012900, 27031186
Timings: 11:00 am to 11:00 pm

Status
11/15, West Patel Nagar, Patel Nagar, Delhi
Phone: 25886692, 25886635
Timings: 11:00 am to 11:00 pm

Suzie Wong
7, Sethi Bhawan, Rajendra Place, Delhi
Phone: 25718528, 25820140
Timings: 12:00 pm to 3:00 pm, 7:00 pm to 11:00 pm

The Chinese
F-14/15, Middle Circle, Connaught Place, Delhi Phone: 23708888, 65398888
Timings: 12:30 pm to 11:30 pm

Yo China, B-7, Vasant Lok, Vasant Vihar, Delhi. Phone: 26151919.
Timings: 12:00 pm to 11:00 pm

Zen
B25, Connaught Place, Delhi
Phone: 23357455
Timings: 10:30 am to midnight

Multi Cuisine

Buzz
17, Commercial Centre, First Floor, Saket, Delhi Phone: 26533999, 26533000
Timings: 12:30 pm to midnight
(Happy Hours: 4.00 p.m. - 7.45 p.m.)

GayLord
16-B, Regal Building, Connaught Place, Delhi Phone: 23360717
Timings: 12:00 pm to 3:00 pm, 7:00 pm to 11:00 pm

Host
F 8, Connaught Place, Delhi
Phone: 23316381, 23316576
Timings: 10:00 am to 11:00 pm

Haowin
82, Pratap Nagar, Kiran Jyoti Complex, First Floor, Mayur Vihar Phase I, Delhi Phone: 22750141, 22795552
Timings: 12:00 pm to 11:00 pm

Hakka
0-27, West Patel Nagar, Patel Nagar, Delhi
Phone: 25875657, 25875104, 25874299, Timings: 11:00 am to 11:00 pm

Hubb
M2k, Multiplex, Sector-3, Rohini, Delhi
Phone: 27940404
Timings: 12:00 pm to midnight

Jupiter
32/33, Near Petrol Pump, Jwala Heri Market, Paschim Vihar, Delhi
Phone: 25289998, 25289999
Timings: 11:00 am to midnight

Jugal Bandi
1st Roor Market, Choudhary Kishan Chand Shopping Complex, Jawala Heri Market, Paschim Vihar, Delhi
Phone: 65403825, 25255678
Timings: 11:00 am to 11:00 pm

Lido Diners
M-38, Outer Circle, Opposite Shanker Market, Connaught Place, Delhi
Phone: 9810527567, 41536000, 41536196
Timings: 12:00 pm to midnight

Laid Backwaters
Qutab Hotel, Shaheed Jeet Singh Marg, Qutab Institutional Area, Delhi
Phone: 41688962, 41200040, 9811507337
Timings: 12:30 pm to 3:00 pm, 7:30 pm to 1:00 am

Thai

Bell Peppers
B-1/6, Ashok Vihar Phase II, Ashok Vihar, Delhi Phone: 27444512, 27444513
Timings: 11:30 am to 3:00 pm, 7:30 pm to 11:00 pm

Beijing Garden
Road No. 31, Punjabi Bagh Extension, Delhi Phone: 9212037555, 25223469
Timings: 11:00 am to midnight

Chilli Season
47 Defence Colony Market, Defence Colony Market, Defence Colony, Delhi Phone: 24618358, 24643362
Timings: 12:00 pm to 3:00 pm, 7:00 pm to 11:00 pm

Eatopia
Lodhi Road, Delhi Phone: 51220000
Timings: 12:00 pm to 11:00 pm

The Spice Route
Hotel Imperial, Janpath, Connaught Place, Delhi Phone: 23341234
Timings: 12:30 pm to 3:00 pm, 7:30 pm to 11:45 pm

Kylin
24, Basant Lok, Vasant Vihar, Delhi
Phone: 41669799, 41669178
Timings: 12:00 pm to midnight

Italian

Marco Polo
Bistro, 12, Hauz Khas Village, Hauz Khas, Delhi Phone: 26853857, 26852227
Timings: 12:30 pm to 3:00 pm, 7:00 pm to midnight

Ploof
13, Main Market, Lodhi Road, Delhi
Phone: 24634666, 24649026
Timings: 12:00 pm to 3:00 pm, 7:00 pm to 11:00 pm

Q'BA
E-42143, Inner Circle, Connaught Place, Delhi
Phone: 41512888
Timings: 12:00 pm to midnight

Red Coral
426, Ghitorni, Main Mehrauli-Gurgaon Road, Mehrauli, Delhi   Phone: 26501050, 26501060, 30997246-47
Timings: 11:00 am to 11:00 pm

United Coffee House
E E-15, Connaught Place, Delhi
Phone: 23411697, 23416075
Timings: 9:30 am to 11:30 pm

FAST FOOD

Fast food snack bars are now becoming a dime a dozen in the capital but the originators of this American style of food service were the Nirula group. They have a block of snack bars and restaurants that include self-service and table-service snack bars, a pizza parlour, a salad bar, an ice cream parlour, a Chinese restaurant etc.

Haldirams – a household name in Indian sweets and snacks - has a huge restaurant in Delhi near Chandni Chowk. They serve up good, clean, street snacks - proper Indian fare. The "pav bhaji" which is a flavoursome snack of mixed vegetables served up on piping hot fried bread – is a speciality here.

Several international food chains – like Macdonalds, Pizza Hut, KFC and Subway have opened their outlets in Delhi. Most of these places serve pizzas, burgers and salads as well as Indian Kababs and Tandoori items.

And there are of course the leisurely coffee houses where it has long been the tradition for intellectuals (self-styled and otherwise) and students to gather for coffee and chatter.

Fast Food

AMERICAN PIE, Asian Games Village Complex, Tel: 6447280

CAFÉ 100, Connaught place, Tel: 3350051

CROSSANTS ETC, Basant lok Complex, Tel: 3710856

KENTS, 29 Defence Colony Market, Tel:4623847

SLICE OF ITALY, Tel: 687337/606860

STICKY FINGERS, Tel: 4622247

WENGER'S, A-16, Connaught Place, Tel: 3324373

NIRULAS
Connaught place, Tel: 3322419/3315617
Chanakya Cinema Complex, Tel 602116
Defence Colony, Tel 4621592
East of Kailash,Tel: 6424487
Kamla Nagar, Karol Bagh, Tel:5746050
Vasant Vihar, Tel: 6887756
Noida, Tel: 8926513
WIMPY'S, Janpath, Tel: 33313910

All HEAVENS PARTY HALL
-97, Wazirpur Ring Road, Tel: 712453

DOMINO'S PIZZA
Sagar Center, Gujranwala, Tel:746565

KABABE-E-BAHAR CHICKEN CORNER
Model Town- 11, Tel:7246670

Coffee Shops

BLOOMS, The park Royal, Tel: 6223344

CAFÉ, Hyatt Regency, Tel: 6181234

CARAVAN, Ashok Yatri Niwas,Tel: 3324511

CANA CONA, Vasant Continental, Tel:6871100

CLUB CAFÉ, Hans Plaza, Tel:3316868

CARDENIA, Samrat, Tel: 603030

GARDEN PARTY, Imperial, Tel: 3341234

GARDEN TERRACE, Oberoi Maidens, Tel:2525464

ISFAHAN, Taj Palace, Tel: 6110202

LA BRASSERIE, Le Meridien, Tel: 3710101

LA PLAZA, Le Meridien, Tel: 3710101

LE CAFÉ, Best Western Surya, Tel: 6835070

LUMBINI, Siddhartha, Tel: 5762501

MACHAN, Taj Mahal, Tel: 3016162

NYC, Radisson, Tel:6129191

OPEN HOUSE, Janpath, Tel: 3340070

PALM COURT, Kanishka, Tel: 3344422

PALMYRA, Bristol, Tel: 91- 356030

PICKWICK, Claridges, Tel: 3010211

PORTICO, The Park , Tel: 3322419

SAMOVAR, Ashok, Tel: 6110101

THE COFFEE SHOP, Ashok, Tel:6110101

THE PALMS, The Oberoi, Tel: 4363030

THE PAVILLION, Maurya Sheraton, Tel:6112233

THE RENDEZVOUS, Inter- Continental, Tel: 3320101

THE GRILL, Qutab, Tel: 6521314

TIFFANY, The Connaught, Tel: 3364225

ENTERTAINMENT

SHOPPING MALLS

Ansal Plaza
HUDCO Place, Khel Gaon Marg Andrews Ganj, New Delhi - 110 049
Phone: 26261305, 26255532

AEZ Square Mall
G-1, Community Centre, Vikas Puri, New Delhi - 110018

CTC Plaza
(Garment Mall) North Square Mall G1 & G2, Ground Floor, Netaji Subhash Place Pitampura,
New Delhi - 110 088 Phone: 47020044

Cross-River Mall 9B & 9C, Central Business, Shahdara, New Delhi - 110095.

Mamram Majesty Mall Plot No. 2 Guru Harkishan Marg Road No. 43, Pitampura, New Delhi - 110083
Phone: 2596 6688, Fax: 2547 8186

Mamram Magic Mall Plot No. 4, CS / OCF Sector - 24, Phase - III Rohini, New Delhi - 110085 Phone: 554 60213

Metro Walk Mall Sector 10, Rohini, Adjacent to Rithala Metro Station, New Delhi 110041
Phone: 27573480, 27574061

North Square Mall F-1, 2,3 Netaji Subhash Place, Pitampura, Near T.V. Tower, New Delhi
Phone: 47049061

North Ex Mall Sector-9, Near Kadambiri C.G.H.S. Rohini, New Delhi - 110085
Phone: 554 60213

Vasant Square Mall Plot No.- A, Community Centre, Sector-B, Pocket-5, Vasant Kunj, New Delhi - 110 070
Phone: 51523164-168

CINEMA HALLS

Amba Satya Nagar, Near Ghanta Ghar, Kamla Nagar, Delhi -110007 Phone: 23826000

Alpana Cinema Ring Road Model Town, Delhi 110009
Phone: 27413104

Chanakya Theatre Vinay Marg, Chanakyapuri, New Delhi 110021 Phone: 2467 4009, 2467 0423

Filmistan Model Basti, Rani Jhansi Road, Karol Bagh, New Delhi 110005 Phone: 23673821, 23673120

Fun Cinema East Centre, Plot No. 10,Main Vikas Marg, Laxminagar District Centre, New Delhi - 110092 Phone: 32583137

Golcha 3630, Netaji Subhash Chander Marg,
New Delhi - 110 002 Phone: 2326 5192, 2325 0945

Liberty 19-B, New Rohtak Road, Karol Bagh,
New Delhi 110060 Phone: 28712998, 28711800

Moti Diwan Hall Road Chandni Chowk, New Delhi - 110 002 Phone: 2386 0383

M2K 4, Community Centre, Road No. 44, Pitampura, New Delhi - 110034 Phone: 30908362

Odeon D-Block, Connaught Place, New Delhi - 110001
Phone: 41515050, 41517899

PVR Plaza H- Block, Connaught Place, New Delhi - 110001 Phone: 5151 3391, 9632000787

Regal Connaught Circus, Connaught Place, New Delhi - 110001 Phone: 2336 2245, 2336 1583

Rachna 2, Rajendra Place, Pusa Road, Karol Bagh,
New Delhi - 110 002 Phone: 25713586

Shiela Theatre D.B. Gupta Road, Delhi - 110 055
Phone: 23672100

Shakuntalam Theatre Near Gate No.2, Pragati Maidan, New Delhi - 110001
Phone: 23371849, 23318143

Sangam Sector 9, R K Puram, New Delhi 110021
Phone: 26172442

Sapna 54, Suraj Parbat, East of Kailash, New Delhi 110065 Phone: 26431787

ART GALLERIES

Dhoomimal Art Gallery 8 A Connaught Place, New Delhi - 110001 Phone: 2332 4492, 2332 8316
Opening Hours: 11.00 am to 6.00 pm

Creativity Art Gallery 29, Hauz Khas Village,
New Delhi - 110016 Phone: 2652 9392, 3095 2077

Gallery Espace 16, Community Centre, New Friends Colony, New Delhi 110065
Phone: 2632 6267

India International Centre 40 Max Mueller Marg,
New Delhi - 110003 Phone: 2461 9431
Opening Hours: 9.00 am to 10.00 pm

Lalit Kala Akademi Rabindra Bhawan, Ferozshah Road, New Delhi - 110001
Phone: 2338 7241 2338 7242
Opening Hours: 11.00 am to 7.00 pm

Studio Vasant Art Gallery 39 G.F.Paschimi Marg, Vasant Vihar, New Delhi 110057 Phone: 4601 2292

BAR & PUBS

Bacchus
5, Basant Lok, Vasant Vihar, New Delhi 110057 Phone: 2615 6895

Beach Bar
29, Community Centre PVR Complex, Saket, New Delhi - 110017 Phone: 26517356

Djinns
Hotel Hyatt Regency, Bhikaiji Cama Place, Ring Road, New Delhi Phone: 26791234, Fax: 26791122

Geoffrey's
Ansal Plaza, Khel Gaon Marg, New Delhi 110049 Phone: 26264515

H2O
The Ambassador Hotel - New Delhi Sujan Singh Park, Cornwallis Road, New Delhi - 110003 Phone: 2463 2600

Ministry of Sound
The Pyramid, 11 LSC Sector C Pocket 6/7, Vasant Kunj, New Delhi 110070 Phone: 46045319

My Kind of Place
Taj Palace, Sardar Patel Marg, Diplomatic Enclave, New Delhi - 110021 Phone: 26110202,

Rick's
The Taj Mahal Hotel 1, Mansingh Road, New Delhi - 110011 Phone: 23026162

Ssteel
The Ashok Hotel, 50 B, Chanakyapuri, New Delhi - 110021 Phone: 2611 0101, 2611 6161

Trafalgar's
Chattarpur Road, Near Chattarpur Mandir, Mehrauli, New Delhi Phone: 2630 1111

Thugs
Broadway Hotel, 4/15 Asaf Ali Road, New Delhi - 110002 Phone: 2327 3821

Turquoise Cottage
81/3, Adchini Sri Aurbindo Marg, New Delhi Phone: 2685 3896

Tusker's
Bangla Sahib Road, New Delhi - 110001 Phone: 42500200, Fax: 42500300

The Float
Park Royal Hotel, International Trade Tower, New Delhi - 110019 Phone: 2622 3344

Vintage
Ring Road, Lajpat Nagar, New Delhi 110024 Phone: 2643 6451

GETTING AROUND THE CITY

CALL TAXIS

Metered taxis, a better class of vehicles called the 'private taxi' and chauffeur-driven air-conditioned cars and limousines are all available for hire.

Taxi stands are located near the hotels, major shopping centres and road junctions.

There are scores of private and luxury taxi operators, some near the hotels, others whom you can contact throught the hotels or your travel agents. Some of these services are:

24 HOURS TAXI SERVICES

Himachal Taxi Service .... Ph: 26143583
Hardeep Singh Punjab
    Taxi Service .... Ph: 25514865
Ishwar Taxi Service .... Ph: 66338808
Jai Bharat Tourist Taxi Service .... Ph: 26862585,
    26521785
Lucky Tourist Taxi Services Ph: 29254510,
    29251443
New Lodhi Taxi Service .... Ph: 24362821,
    24365266
Panwar Taxi Services .... Ph: 66357829
Prem Tourist Taxi Service . Ph: 26252170
Surjit Tourist Taxi Services Ph: 66358193
Ranjeet Taxi Services ... Ph: 9811415873,
    9313786378

CAR RENTALS

Ajay Tour & Travels .... Ph: 66338745
Apollo Travels .... Ph: 66227213
City Tour Travel .... Ph: 66360238
Globe Travel Co .... Ph: 66358606
Mahalaxmi Travels .... Ph: 66225987
Mehta Tours & Travels ...... Ph: 66360417
Mesco Tours & Travels ...... Ph: 66266978
Northern Tour & Travels ... Ph: 66362030
Shivam Tour N Travels ...... Ph: 66362951
Sam India Travels .... Ph: 66264647

IMPORTANT BUS ROUTES

Time Table of Air Conditioned Low Floor Buses operating in Delhi

Route No.	Departure Time		Via
419	From Ambedkar Nagar Terminal	From Railway Station	Sheikh Sarai Phase-II, MCKR Hospital, Pant Nagar, Mathura Road, Bahadur Shah Zafar Marg, Red Fort.
	0606	0730	
	0654	0818	
	0924	1051	
	1015	1142	
	1433	1606	
	1500	1630	
	1800	1930	
	1824	1954	

Route No.	Departure Time		Via
423	From Ambedkar Nagar Terminal	From Mori Gate Terminal	Sheikh Sarai Phase-II, MCKR Hospital, Pant Nagar, Mathura Road, Bahadur Shah Zafar Marg, Delhi Gate, Raj Ghat Ring Road, ISBT.
	0739	0939	
	0827	1000	
	1103	1239	
	1154	1327	
	1548	1745	
	1612	1809	
	1915	2057	
	1939	2109	

Route No.	Departure Time		Via
440	From Tara Apartment	From New Delhi Railway Station Gate No.-2	Kalkaji DDA Flats, D.B. Gupta College, Nehru Place, LSR College, Mool Chand, Andrews Ganj, J.L. Nehru Stdium, S. Bharti Marg, Shahjahan Road, K.G. Marg.
	0700	0830	
	0800	0930	
	0830	1000	
	1000	1200	
	1100	1300	
	1200	1330	
	1520	1715	
	1620	1750	
	1650	1820	
	1845	2015	
	1940	2110	
	2010	2140	

Route No.	Departure Time		Via
460	From Badar Pur X-ing	From New Delhi Railway Station Gate No.-2	Sarita Vihar Xing, Mathura Road, Ashram, Ring Road, AIIMS, S.J. Madrasa, Tuglak Road, Krishi Bhawan, P.S. Parliament.
	0620	0926	
	0748	1110	
	1136	1306	
	1540	1318	
	1555	1335	
	1604	1742	
	1625	2030	
	1640	2125	
	1952	2138	

Route No.	Departure Time		Via
502	From Mehrauli	From Railway Station	Qutab, Police Traning School, I.I.T Gate, AIIMS, S.J. Madrasa, Prithvi Raj. Road, Shahjahan Road, India Gate, Tilak Marg, ITO (BSZ Marg), Red Fort.
	0700	0832	
	0754	0926	
	0906	1038	
	0954	1144	
	1124	1256	
	1136	1408	
	1518	1644	
	1606	1738	
	1718	1850	
	1812	2002	
	1936	2108	
	2048	2202	

Route No.	Departure Time		Via
522	From Ambedkar Nagar Terminal	From New Delhi Railway Station Gate No.-2	Sheikh Sarai Phase-II, MCKR Hospital, Andrews Ganj, J.L. Nehru Stdium, S. Bharti Marg, Shahjahan Road, K.G. Marg.
	0835	0810	
	0930	0955	
	1143	1008	
	1159	1030	
	1218	1305	
	1850	1730	
	1943	1830	

Route No.	Departure Time		Via
534	From Nehru Place	From Anand Vihar ISBT	
	0655	0815	PTS Press Enclave Road, Chirag Delhi, Nehru Place, Holy Family X-ing, Maharani Bagh, Sarai Kale Khan ISBT, East Nizamuddin Bridge, Mother Dairy, Balco Apartment, Hasan Pur Depot.
	0710	0830	
	0725	0845	
	0740	0900	
	1505	1240	
	1520	1300	
	1530	1310	
	1550	1320	
	1620	1340	
	From Qutab	1625	
		1640	
	1025	1700	
	1040	1730	
	1110	1800	
	1120	2110	
	1835	2120	
	1855	2130	
	1910	2140	
	1935	2150	
	1950	2220	
	2010	2230	
	2025		

Route No.	Departure Time		Via
604	From Basant Kunj Sec-A	From New Delhi Railway Station Gate No.-2	Kishan Garh, Manav Sathli School, Power House, Nelson Mandela Marg, Swami Malai Mandir, Moti Bagh, Shanti Path, Teen Murti, Krishi Bhawan, P.S. Parliament.
	0830	1730	
	0900	1815	

Route No.	Departure Time		Via
724	From Nehru Place	From Uttam Nagar Terminal	Sant Nagar, Lady Shri Ram College, Andrews Ganj, AIIMS, R.K. Puram Sec-12 (Ring Road), Dhaula Kuan, RR Line, Thimia Marg, Kirby Place, Sadar Cantt Rly. Station, Sagar Pur, Janak Puri C2-B, Janak Puri C-I.
	0630	0815	
	0730	0915	
	1025	1210	
	1125	1310	
	1440	1625	
	1540	1725	
	1810	2020	
	1910	2120	

TOURIST BUS SERVICES

Delhi Transport Corporation (DTC) operates daily sightseeing tours from Scindia House. The fare of Delhi Darshan Service is Rs.100/- for adults and Rs.50/- for children between the age group of 5 – 12 years. Besides, DTC has also introduced AC bus for Delhi Darshan service on Sundays and Holidays. The fare of AC bus is Rs.200/- for adult and Rs.100/- for children between the age group of 5 –12 years. However, children will not be entitled to a seat in the bus. The Delhi Darshan ticket will be valid in all City Services on the pattern of DTC Green Card.

The time of journey is from 09.15 to 17.45 hrs.

The tourist bus starts from DTC Office Scindia House, then pickup tourists from Information Kiosk of Delhi Tourism Baba Kharak Singh Marg and thereafter from India Tourism Development Corporation (ITDC) Office at Janpath for onward journey to the tourist places as per the following program:

Red Fort - 45 minutes (Halting Time)

Raj Ghat (India Gate by Pass) - 20 minutes

Birla Mandir - 30 minutes
Qutab Minar - 45 minutes
Lotus Temple - 45 minutes.
Humanyun's Tomb - 45 minutes
Akshardham Temple (Swami Narain Temple) - Dropping only.

Route to be followed (VIA)

Delhi Gate, Shanti Van, Tilak Mark, Akbar Road, Sansad Marg, Shanti Path, Siri Aurbindo Marg, Press Enclave Road, Out Ring Road (Nehru Place), Modi Floor Mill, Ring Road, Mathura Road, Lodhi Road, Pragati Maidan, Nizamuddin Yamuna Bridge, Laxmi Nagarl, DDU Marg and Connaught Place.

For Reservation and Enquiry one can contact phone No.28844192 Extn. 244, Delhi Darshan Counter,Scindia House, Connaught Place.

DELHI METRO RAILWAY

Delhi Metro, a project under taken by Delhi Metro Rail Corporation has set records in both time and efficiency, in its construction phase throughout the city. The project also seeks to provide its commuters with very high levels of security and safety.

The first phase of the project which is about to be completed is already up and running with it's trains setting international standards for public transport in India.

Metro Phase 1
LINE 1
SHAHDARA to RITHALA via KASHMERE GATA
LINE 2
CENTERAL SECRETARIAT to DELHI UNIVERSITY via RAJIV CHOWK and KASHMERE GATE
LINE 3
BARAKHAMBA ROAD to DWARKA via RAJIV CHOWK
Commuters willing to change lines can interchange at Kashmere gate and Rajiv Chowk
Timings: **6 AM to 10 PM**

Last Trains available at Kashmere Gate Interchange

22:10 Hrs for going towards Rithala

22:27 Hrs for going towards Shahdara

22:38 Hrs for going towards CentralSecretariat

22:54 Hrs for going towards Vishwavidyalaya **Last Trains available at Rajiv Chowk Interchange**

22:02 Hrs for going towards Dwarka

22:39 Hrs for going toward Barakhamba

22:46 Hrs for going towards Vishwavidyalaya & Central Secretariat

TOURIST INFORMATION CENTERS

The Government of India has a tourist office at 88 Janpath, New Delhi, Tel: +91 11 332 0005.

The office is open Monday to Friday from 9:00 am to 6:00 pm and on Saturday from 9:00 am to 2:00 pm. Information is not displayed and therefore tourists should enquire first.

There are also tourist information offices at the airport, and the following places:

Delhi Tourism & Transportation Development Coporation

Baba Kharak Singh Marg, Tel: 011-23365358/23363607

N-36, Middle Circle, Connaught Place, Tel: 011-23315322/23314229

Government of India Tourist Office., Tel: 23320005/8

Indira Gandhi International Airport Terminal-II , Tel: 011-25691213

Indira Gandhi Domestic Airport Terminal –I, Tel: 011-25665609/25665126

New Delhi Railway Station, Tel:011- 23732374

Old Delhi Railway Station, Tel: 011-23961083

Nizamuddin Railway Station, Tel:011- 24359748

Delhi Cantonment Enquiry:011-25693846

Transport Office, West Kidwai Nagar, Sri Aurobindo Marg, Tel:011-24674153/26884312

Inter State Bus Terminal, Tel:011-23867042/23868836

India Tourism Development Corporation (ITDC), Scope Complex, Core 8, Lodhi Road, Tel:011-24360303

Ministry of Tourism's Control Room, 88 Janpath, Tel:011-23320342

OTHER STATE TOURISM OFFICES

Andaman and Nicobar Islands, F-105, Curzon Road Hostel, Kasturba Gandhi Marg, Tel: 3782904

Andhra Pradesh Tourism, 1 Ashoka Road, Tel:3381293

Assam Tourism, Baba Kharag Singh Marg, Tel: 345897

Bihar, Kanishka Shopping Plaza, Tel: 3723371

Chandigarh, Harish Chander Mathur Lane, K.G.Marg, Tel: 3353359

Goa, Goa Sadan, 18 Amrita Shergil Marg, Tel: 4629967/462968

Gujarat, Baba K.S.Marg, Tel: 3732107

Harayana, Chandralok Building, 36 Janpath, Tel: 3324911

Himachal Pradesh, Chandralok Building, 36 Janpath, Tel: 3325320

Jammu & Kashmir, Kanishka Shopping Plaza, 19,Ashok Road, Tel: 3325373/3716081

Kerala, Kanishka Shopping Plaza, 19, Ashok Road, Tel: 3325373/ 3716081

Karnataka, Baba K.S.Marg, Tel: 343862

Madhya Pradesh, Kanishka Shopping Plaza, 19, Ashok Road, Tel: 3321187

Maharashtra, Baba K.S.Marg, Tel: 343862

Meghalaya, 9 Aurangzeb Road, Tel: 3014417

Orissa, Baba K.S.Marg, Tel: 344580

Rajasthan, Bikaner House, Near India Gate, Tel: 3383837/338925

Sikkim, 14 Panchsheel Marg, Chanakyapuri, Tel: 3015346

Tamil Nadu, Baba K.S. Marg, Tel: 3735427

Uttar Pradesh, Chandralok Buliding, 36 Janpath, Tel:3322251

West Bengal, Baba K.S.Marg, Tel: 3732840

AIR LINES

Airlines that operate flights to and from Delhi:

International Airlines

Aeroflot - Russian Airlines, City off: 011-3312843/0426,Airport: 011- 5653510

Air Canada, City off: 011-3720014/15 / 43, Airport: 011- 5652850

Air France, City off: 011- 3738004/05, Airport: 011- 5652099

Air India, City off: 011-3736446 / 7 /8, Airport: 011- 5652050

Sri Lankan Airlines City off: 011-3368843 /45, Airport: 011- 5652957

Air Mauritius, City off:011-37311225/1534/1537, Airport:011-5652050

Air Ukraine, City off: 011-6867545, Airport: 011-5653514

All Nippon Airways, City off: 011-3736980/82/83

American Airlines, City off: 011-3325876

Ariana Afghan Airlines, City off: 011-3312478

Austrian Airlines, City off: 011-3350125 /6

Biman Bangladesh Airlines, City off: 011-3354401/2/3/4,Airport: 011-5652943

British Airways, City off: 011-3327428, Airport: 5652077/2908

Cathay Pacific, City off: 011-3323332 /3323919

Delta Airlines, City off :011-3325222/5073, Airport: 011-5653029

Druk Air - The Royal Bhutan Airlines, City off: 011-3310990, Airport: 5653207

Egypt Airlines, City off: 011-3731896

EL– AL Israel Airlines, City off: 011-3357965

Ethiopian Airlines, City off: 011-3312302/03, Airport: 011-5653739/40

Emirates, City off: 011-3324665/4803, Airport: 011-5696861

Finnair, City off: 011-3315454

Gulf Air, City off:011- 3324293, Airport: 5652065

Iberia, City off: 011-3367989

Iran Air- The Airline of the Islamic Republic of Iran, City Off: 011-6889123/606471

Iraqi Airways, City off: 011-3318742, Airport:011- 5652011

Jal Japan Airlines, City off: 3324922, Airport: 5653941/42

Kazakhstan Airlines, City Off: 011-3367889, Arport: 011-5652695/2011

Kenya Airways - The Pride of Africa, City off: 011-3357747/3721141

KLM – Royal Dutch Airlines, City off: 011-3357747/3721141 Airport:011- 5652715

Korean Air, City off: 011-3315454/3721913

Kuwait Airways, City off:011- 3354373/77, Airport:011- 5652295

Kryghyzstan Airlines, City off: 011-3368332/8738

Lufthansa, City off:011- 3323310, Airport:011- 5652328

Malaysia Airlines, City off: 011-3324308, Airport 011-5652395

PIA – Pakistan Intenational Airlines, City off: 011-3737791/2/3, Airport 0ff: 011-5652841

Royal Jordanian, City 0ff:011-3320635/7418, Airport :011-5652478

Royal Nepal Airlines, City off:011- 3321164, Airport:011- 5483876

SAS – Scandinavian Airlines, City off: 011-3352299/3350307, Airport: 011-5653708

Saudi Arabian Airlines, City off: 011-3310464, Airport: 011-5666279

Singapore Airlines, City off:011-3329036/6373, Airport:011- 5653072

South African Airways, City off: 011-3327503/5361/5262

SwissAir, City off: 011-3325511, Airport:011-5652531

Syrian, City off: 011-3738938/9

Tarom - Romanian Air Transport, City off:011-3354422/3/4/5248, Airport: 011-5653711

Thai Airways, City off:011-6239133 /988, Airport: 011-5652413

United, City off:011-3353377/3042, Airport 011-5653910

Uzbekistan Airways, City off: 011-3357939, Airport :011-5652484

Domestic Airlines

Archana Airways Ltd, City off: 011-6842001, Airport: 011-5665854/5519

Jagson Airlines, City off: 011-3721594, Airport: 011-5665545

Jet Airways, City off: 011-6853700, Airport: 011-5665404

Indian Airlines, City off: 011 3719168/3310517
General Enquiry-140   Reservation -141
Arrival- 142   Departure-143

Air Sahara, City off: 011-3326 851, Airport, 011-5665234/5879

UP Airways, City off: 011-4646290/91/92, Airport : 011-5665126/27

ESSENTIAL SERVICES
BANKS

Axis Bank
A-13, Vikas Marg, Swasthya Vihar, Delhi – 110092, Ph: 22014245, 22016630

Bank of Baroda
32,community Centre, PH-1, Naraina Industrial Estate, Delhi – 110028
Ph: 25798092, 25892676

Bank of India
D-80, Main Market, Malviya Nagar, Delhi – 110017, Ph: 26672390, 26672399
Vijaya Building, 1st Floor, 17, Barakhamba Road, Delhi – 110001,
Ph: 28844203, 23736120

Bank of Rajasthan
Hs-5, Main Mkt, Kailash Colony, Delhi – 110048, Ph: 29238986, 32442777
F-42, Kohlapur Road, Kamla Nagar, Delhi – 110007, Ph: 32518348, 32591777

Canara Bank
C-30, commumnity Centre, C Blk, Janak Puri, Delhi – 110058,
Ph: 25573204, 25545731
7, Central Market, north West Avenue, West Avenue Road, Punjabi Bagh, Delhi – 110026, Ph: 25228838, 25228848, 25224648
1487-1497,Fountain, Near Moti Cinema, Chandni Chowk, Delhi - 110006
Ph: 23863721, 23867223, 23865836

HDFC Bank
22, Sunder Nagar Market, Sunder Nagar, Delhi – 110003, Ph: 41507194, 41507195
14, Anand Lok, August Kranti Marg, Andrews Ganj, Delhi – 110049,
Ph: 41740457, 41740458
1907, Opp Gurudwara Sis Ganj, Chandni Chowk, Delhi – 110006, Ph: 23864692, 23864694, 23864698

Indian Bank
2/7,Ground Floor, Desh Bandhu Gupta Road, Pahar Ganj, Delhi – 110055
Ph: 23584391, 23561681
B-1/7,Ground Floor, PH-2, Ashok Vihar, Delhi – 110052, Ph: 27411133, 27411134

Indian Overseas Bank
1/209,Sadar Bazar, Delhi Cantt, Delhi – 110010, Ph: 25693518, 25699904, 25688306
CRPF School, Sec-14, Rohini, Delhi – 110085, Ph: 27565657, 27553876

ICICI Bank
ICICI Bank Tower, N B C C Place, Pragati Vihar, Lodhi Road, Delhi - 110003
Ph: 24390051, 24390052
B-54, Mohatta Towers, B-Block, Community Centre, Janak Puri, Delhi – 110058
Ph: 41718000

Punjab National Bank
Khanpur Branch, Mehrauli Badarpur Road, Mehrauli, Delhi - 110030
Ph: 26088210, 26053148, 26087033
D-17, Anand Niketan, Moti Bagh, Delhi – 110021,Ph: 24112689, 46012858

State Bank of India
Shopping Centre, Mansarover Garden, Delhi – 110015, Ph: 25938438, 25458017
1/18b, Asaf Ali Road, Delhi – 110002,
Ph: 23237223, 23234828, 23233141, 23231422

Union Bank of India
C-32, Dda Commercial Complex, Defence Colony, Delhi – 110024, Ph: 24649581
Post Mangolupuri Kalan,
Mangolpuri, Delhi – 110083,
Ph: 27922593

ATMS

Axis Bank
F-2/25, East Delhi, Krishna Nagar, Delhi - 110051
D-81, Defence Colony, Delhi - 110024
P No-6, Local Shopping Complex, DP-Block, Pitampura, Delhi – 110088

ABN AMRO Bank
C-7, Shopping Complex Facilities, Alaknanda Market, Kalkaji, Delhi - 110019
Shop A-1, Ground Floor, Vikas Tower, Community Centre, Vikas Puri, Delhi - 110018
DDA Shopping Complex, Rajindra Place, Delhi – 110008

Bank of Baroda
A-114, Kamla Nagar Chowk, Shakti Nagar, Delhi - 110007
55, Madhuban Building, Near Main Road, Nehru Place, Delhi - 110019
P No-8 K P, Local Shopping Centre, Pitampura, Delhi – 110088

Bank of Rajasthan
132 Hargobing Enclave, Delhi Gpo, Delhi – 110006
A 1/3 Ground Floor, Main Rohtak Road, Paschim Vihar, Delhi – 110063

Bank of India
Central Ring, P B No-404, Connaught Circus, Delhi - 110001
Paras Cinema Building, Nehru Place, Delhi - 110019
J-2/1, B K Dutta Market, Rajouri Garden, Delhi – 110027

Canara Bank
C-30, Community Centre, C Block, Janak Puri, Delhi - 110058
Shop No-9, Gulmohar Enclave, Community Centre, Green Park, Delhi - 110016
A-9, DDA Shopping Complex, Lajpat Nagar, Delhi – 110024

ICICI Bank
E-568, Part-2, Greater Kailash, Delhi - 110048
A-34, Near Santosh Hotel, Lajpat Nagar, Delhi – 110024
1486, Near Moti Cinema, Chandni Chowk, Delhi – 110006

Indian Bank
C-19, Community Centre, Janak Puri, Delhi - 110058
117, Opp Yamuna Sports Complex, Ram Vihar, Anand Vihar, Delhi – 110092
City Hospital, Pusa Road,
West Patel Nagar, Delhi – 110008

HSBC Bank
G-3, Shakuntala Apartment, 59, Nehru Place, Delhi - 110019
P No-12, Basant Lok, Vasant Vihar, Delhi - 110057
P No-17, Shop No-3, Ground Floor, Community Centre, Saket, Delhi – 110017

HDFC Bank
22, Sunder Nagar Market, Sunder Nagar, Delhi – 110003
14, Anand Lok, August Kranti Marg, Andrews Ganj, Delhi – 110049
A-9, Part-4, Ring Road, Lajpat Nagar, Delhi – 110024

Punjab National Bank
N-46, Gurudwara Road, Karol Bagh, Delhi – 110005
13, Alipur Road, Civil Lines, Delhi – 110054
P No-5, Local Shopping Complex, Block-D, Vasant Vihar, Delhi - 110057

State Bank of India (SBI)
IBP Petrol Pump, Mallia Mandir, Vasant Vihar, Delhi - 110057
6, Part-4, Ring Road, Lajpat Nagar, Delhi - 110024
16/67-68, Faiz Road, Karol Bagh, Delhi – 110005

FOREIGN MONEY EXCHANGE

American Express Bank
Wenger House, Connaught Place, New Delhi - 110001 Ph: 23324119, 51516631-33

Delhi Tourism Foreign Exchange
N-36, Bombay Life Building, Connaught Place, Delhi - 110001
Ph: 23730416, 23315322

Laxnar Forex
11 L, Gopala Tower, Rajindra Place, Delhi - 110008 Ph: 66225243

Sangat Money Exchange Pvt Limited
B-45, Ground Floor, Shivalik, Malviya Nagar, Delhi – 110017 Ph: 66358350

Thomas Cook
Imperial Hotel, Janpath, Delhi – 110001
Ph: 23340564

Weizmann Forex Ltd
M-8, Ground Floor, Punj House, Connaught Place, Delhi – 110001 Ph: 23412034, 23412035

CONSULATES AND EMBASSIES

India, as a growing economy and a world player, is a country where most of the world maintains major diplomatic representation. The bulk of the embassies are in the Chanakyapuri Diplomatic Enclave and Vasant Vihar areas. Many countries maintain cultural organisations – such as libraries, reading rooms and language-teaching centres – in other part of Delhi. Here is some of the representation available in Delhi:

Afghanistan, 5/50, Shantipath, Chanakyapuri, Tel: 011-26883601

Algeria, Be-6/5, Vasant Vihar, Tel:011-26146706

Australia, 1/50 G Shantipath, Chanakyapuri, Tel:011- 26888223

Austria, Ep 13 Chandragupta Marg, Chanakyapuri, Tel:011-26889037/49

Bangladesh, 56 Ring Road, Lajpat nagar II, Tel:011- 26834065

Belgium, 50-N Shantipath, Chanakyapuri, Tel:011-26889851

Bhutan, Chandragupta Marg, Chanakyapuri, Tel:011-26889809/9230

Brazil 8, Aurangzeb Road, Tel:011-23017301

Bulgaria, 16-17 Chandragupta Marg, Chanakyapuri, Tel:011- 26115549

Canada, 7/8 Shantipath, Chanakyapuri, Tel:011-26876500

Chile, 146, Jor Bagh, Tel:011- 24617165

China, 50 D Shantipath, Chanakyapuri, Tel 011-26871585

Cambodia, N-14 Panchsheel Park Tel: 011-26495092

Cuba, E-1/9, Vasant Vihar, Tel:011-26143849

Cyprus, 106, Jor Bagh, Tel: 011-24697503/8

Czechoslovakia, 50 M Niti Marg, Chanakyapuri, Tel:011-26110205

Denmark, 11Aurangzeb Road, Tel:011- 23010900

Egypt, 1/50 M Niti Marg, Chankyapuri, Tel:011-26114096

Ethiopia, 7/50 G, satya Marg, Tel: 011-2611 9513/4

Finland, Nyaya Marg, Tel:011-26115258

France, 2/50E Shantipath, Tel:011-26118790

Germany, 6/50-G Shantipath, Tel:011-26871831

Ghana, 50-N, Satya Marg, Chanakyapuri, Tel:011-26883298

Greece, E-32, Dr. S. Radhakrishnan marg, Chanakyapuri, Tel: 011- 26880700

Iran, 5 Barakhamba Road, Tel:011-23329600

Iraq, E-21-24, Vasant Vihar Tel: 011-26149085/9746

Ireland, 230, Jor Bagh, Tel: 011-24626733

Italy, 50-E, Chandragupta Marg, Tel:011-26114355

Jordan, 30 Golflinks, Tel:011-24653318

Kenya, 34 Vasant Marg, Tel:011-26146537

Kuwait, 5A Shantipath, Chankyapuri, Tel:011-24100791

Lebanon, 26B,Sardar Patel.Marg Tel: 011-23013174

Libya, 22 Golf Links, Tel:011-24697717

Malaysia, 50M Satya Marg, Chanakyapuri, Tel:011-26111291

Mauritius, Jesus & Mary Marg, Chankyapuri, Tel: 011-24102161/62

Mexico, C-8 Anand Niketan, Tel: 011-24117180/81/82

Mongolia, 34 Golflinks, Tel:011-24631728

Myanmar (Baurma) 3/50F Nyaya Marg, Chankyapuri Tel: 011-26889007/8

Nepal, I Barakhmba Road, Tel: 011-23328066/9218

Netherlands, 6/50F Shantipath,
   Chanaklyapuri, Tel:011-26884951
New Zealand, 50-N, Nyaya Marg,
   Tel:011-26883170/26876260
Nigeria, 21 Palam Marg, Vasant Vihar,
   Tel:011-26146221/26146645
Norway, 50-C, Shantipath,
   Tel:011-26873532
Pakistan, 2/50, G Shantipath,
   Chanakyapuri, Tel:011-24676004/8467
Philippines, 50 N Nyaya Marg,
   Chankyapuri, Tel:011-26889091
Poland, 50 M Shantipath,
   Chanakyapuri, Tel:011-26889211
Portugal, 8 Palam Marg, Vasant Vihar,
   Tel 011-26142212
Romania, A-52 Vasant Marg,
   Vasant Vihar, Tel 011-26140447
Saudi Arabia, D-12, South Extn,
   Tel:011-26252470/1
Singapore, E6 Chandragupta,
   Tel:011-26877939
Spain, 16, Sunder Nagar,
   Tel: 011-24359004/5/6/7
Sri Lanka, 27 Kautilya Marg,
   Chanakyapuri, Tel:011-23010201
Switzerland, Nyaya Marg,
   Chanakyapuri, Tel:011-26878372
Thailand, 56 N Nyaya Marg,
   Chankyapuri, Tel:011-26118103/4
United Arab Emirates, Ep-12,
   Chandragupta Marg. Tel:011-26872937
United Kingdom, Shantipath,
   Chanakyapuri, Tel:011-26872161/2822
United States of America,
   Shantipath, Chanakyapuri,
   Tel 011-24198000
USSR, Shantipath, Chanakyapuri,
   Tel 605875, 600022
House of Soviet Culture, 24 Feroze Shah
   Road, Tel 3329102
Venezuela, N114 Panchsheel Park,
   Tel 011-26496913/6535/6783
Vietnam, 17 Kautilya Marg, Chanakyapuri,
   Tel 011-23010532
Yemen, B - 70 Greater Kailash I,
   Tel: 011-26144383
Yugoslavia, 3/50 G Niti Marg.
   Chanakyapuri,Tel:011-26873661/2073
Zambia, C-79, Anand Niketan,
   Tel:011-24101289/92

EMERGENCY PHONE NUMBERS

Accident and Trauma Service 109
Ambulance 102
Fire Service....................................... 101
Missing persons Squad 23276300,
   23261048
Police Control Room 100
Indian Red Cross Society 23711551
Bomb Disposal Squads
   West 26152709
   South West 26152810,801
   North 23962281
   New Delhi 23361231
   Delhi 22512201
Airport
   Domestic 25696535, 25665121
   International 25652011,21,50
   Private Airlines 25675126
Indian Airlines
   General Enquiry 400
   Reservation and Booking Enquiry 1401
   Flight Arrival Information 1402
   Flight Departure Information 1403
Railways
   General Enquiry/ Reservations..... 130
   Railway Reservation
   Enquiry 134,513,351,330
   Centralised Railway Enquiry 1330
Bus Services
   Inter-State Enquiry at Kashmiri
   Gate Terminus   22960290,22968836
   Inter-State Enquiry at Sarai Kale Khan
   Terminus 24698343,24638092
   Inter-State Enquiry at Anand Vihar
   Terminus - 22148097
Telephones Services
   Directory Enquiry 197
   Telephone Complaint 198
   Internet Customer Care 1504
   Change Number Hindi 1951
                     English 1952
Tourist Information
   India Tourism Development
   Corporation 23415331,23412330,
   23719039
   Tourism Departments Delhi
   (DTDC) 23363607,23365358
   Tourist Information Service 1363
   Dial a Cab/Car Help line .. 1920,1929
   Transport Arrangements
   23320331,2336
   Tours Department
  23748115,23748164-65

HEALTHCARE

HOSPITALS

All India Institute Of Medical Sciences (AIIMS) – Ph: 26588500, 26588700

Ambedkar Hospital – Ph: 27055585

Anand Hospital – Ph: 22750380, 22795237

B.L.Kapoor Memorial Hospital – Ph: 25719282, 25742342, 25720368

Bansal Hospital – Ph: 46583333

Delhi Heart & Lung Institute – Ph: 42999999, 23538351-8

Dharmashila Cancer Hospital & Research Centre – Ph: 43066666, 43066688

Escorts Heart Institute & Research Centre – Ph: 26825000, 26825001

Guru Teg Bahadur Hospital – Ph: 22586262

Hindu Rao Hospital – Ph: 23932362

Indraprastha Apollo Hospital – Ph: 26925858 / 26925801

Jeevan Anmol Hospital – Ph: 22750380, 22795237

Kalawati Saran Children's Hospital – Ph: 23344160, 23365792, 23344147

Kolmet Hospital – Ph: 25752056, 25863013

Max Hospital – Ph: 2735 1844

Moolchand K R Hospital – Ph: 4200 0000

Metro Hospital & Heart Institute – Ph: 26237962, 63

National Heart Institute – Ph: 26414156, 26414157, 26414251

Ram Manohar Lohia Hospital – Ph: 23365525, 23365988

Sir Ganga Ram Hospital – Ph: 25735205, 25861463

Sankhwar Hospital – Ph: 22612455, 22612400

Sant Parmanand Hospital – Ph: 23981260, 23994401

Venu Eye Institute & Research Centre – Ph: 2925 1155

BLOOD BANKS

All India Institute of Medical Sciences (AIIMS) – Ph: 26588500, 26588700

Bajaj Blood Bank – Ph: 28712849

Batra Hospital & Medical Research Centre – Ph: 26056148, 26056153, 26057154

Blood Bank Organisation – Ph: 25721870, 25711055

CPC Blood Bank – Ph: 26834101

Indian Red Cross Society – Ph: 23711551

Lions Blood Bank – Ph: 9810010954

Rotary Blood Bank – Ph: 29054066, 29054067, 29962078

Sunil Blood Bank and Transfusion Center – Ph: 46507646

Sir Ganga Ram Hospital – Ph: 25735205, 25861463

AMBULANCE SERVICES

Apollo Air Ambulance Service – Ph: 9891486406

Ayushman Ambulance Services – Ph: 9810224875, 9911700900

Delhi Ambulance Services – Ph: 25791387

Green Line Ambulance Service – Ph: 66359326

Help line Ambulance Services (24 Hrs) – Ph: 24351358, 24358836

Kapoor Ambulance Service – Ph: 26287670

Rana Ambulance Services – Ph: 66359393

Ravindra Ambulance Services Ph: 26055535

St John Ambulance Brigade Ph: 23322237, 23720143

Sahara Ambulance Service – Ph: 25498963

24-HOUR PHARMACIES

All India Institute of Medical Sciences (AIIMS) – Ph: 26588500, 26588700

Apollo Pharmacy – Ph: 41626200

Batra Medical Corner – Ph: 25860247

Gulati Medical Store – Ph: 22301640, 22308275

Kolmet Chemist – Ph: 25786165, 25752056

Sant Parmanand Hospital – Ph: 23981260,

ACCOMMODATION

There is no dearth of accommodation in Delhi. The frequent international meets and summits held here have resulted in a tremendous increase in the number of hotels in the city. There is accommodation available to suit every purse – the newest type being the private guesthouses.

Luxury/ 5 Star Deluxe Hotels

THE IMPERIAL
1, Janpath, New Delhi-1
Tel: 011-23341234 Fax:011-23342255
E-mail: luxury@theimperialindia.com.

THE OBEROI
Dr.Zakir Hussain Road, New Delhi-3
Tel: 011-24363030 Fax:011-24360484
E-mail: reservations@oberoidel.com

THE TAJ MAHAL HOTEL
No.1, Man Singh Road, New Delhi-11
Tel: 011-23026162
Fax: 011- 23026070
E-mail: tmhbe@tajhotels.com

THE TAJ PALACE HOTEL
Sardar Patel Marg, Diplomatic Enclave, New Delhi-21
Tel:011-26110202
Fax:011-26110808/ 26884848
E-mail: palace.delhi@tajhotels.com

HOTEL MAURYA SHERATON
Diplomatic Enclave, S.P. Marg, New Delhi-21
Tel: 011-26112233 Fax:011-26113333
E-mail: mauryaguest@hotmail.com

HYATT REGENCY
Bhikaji Cama Place, Ring road, New Delhi-66
Tel: 011-26791234 Fax: 011-26791024
E-mail: hrdelhi@hyattintl.com

LE MERIDIEN
Windsor Place, Janpath, New Delhi-1
Tel: 011-23710101 Fax: 011-23714545
E-mail: info@lemeridien-newdelhi.com

GRAND HYATT
Nelson Mandela Road, Vasant Kunj Phase-11, New Delhi-70
Tell:011-26771234   Fax: 011-26705891
E-mail: reservation@unisonhotels.com

GRAND INTERCONTINENTAL
Barakhamba Avenue, Connaught Place, New Delhi-1
Tel: 011-23411001/ 51511001
Fax: 011- 23412233
E -mail: newdelhi@interconti.com

CENTAUR HOTEL
Indira Gandhi International Airport, New Delhi-37
Tel: 011-25652223/25696660
Fax: 011-25652256/25652239
E-mail: centaur@ndf.vsnl.net.in

INTERCONTINENTAL EROS NEHRU PLACE
S-2, American Plaza, International Trade Tower, Nehru Place, New Delhi –19
Tel: 011-51223344
Fax: 011-26239029
E- mail: del-nehruplace@interconti.com

ASHOK HOTEL
Diplomatic Enclave, 50-B, Chanakyapuri, New Delhi-21
Tel: 011-26110101
Fax: 011-26873216/ 26876060
E-mail: ashoknd@ndb.vsnl.net.in

CROWNE PLAZA SURYA
New Friends Colony, New Delhi -65
Tel: 011-26835070
Fax: 011-26837758
E-mail: suryahotsales@vsnl.net

JAYPEE VASANT CONTINENTAL
Vasant Vihar, New Delhi-57
Tel: 011-26148800/1177
Fax: 011-26145959/26148900
E-mail: hvc@del3.vsnl.net.in

RADISSON HOTEL
National Highway 8, New Delhi-37
Tel: 011-26779191
Fax: 011-26779090
E-mail: raddel@del2.vsnl.net.in

THE PARK HOTEL
15, Parliament Street, New Delhi-1
Tel: 011-23743000
Fax: 011-23744000
E-mail: gm.del@theparkhotels.com

UPPAL'S ORCHID – AN ECOTEL HOTEL
NH-8 Near IGI Airport, New Delhi -37
Tel: 011-51511515
Fax: 011-51511516
E-mail: info@ uppalsorchidhotel.com

5 Star Hotels

HOTEL SAMRAT
Kautilya Marg, Chanakyapuri,
New Delhi -21
Tel: 011-26110606
Fax: 011-26887047/24679056
E-mail: smart21@ ndb.vsnl.net.in

JAYPEE SIDDHARTH
3, Rajendra Place, New Delhi-8
Tel: 011-25762501
Fax: 011-25781016
E-mail: js@jaypeehotels.com

QUTAB HOTEL
Shaheed Jeet Singh Marg, New Delhi-16
Tel: 011-26521010/26521234
Fax: 011-26968287
E-mail: qutab@del3.vsnl.net.in

RADISSON MBD HOTEL
L-2, Sector 18, Noida- 1
Tel: 0120-2515333
Fax:0120-2515444
E-mail: reservations@radissonmbd.com

THE AMBASSADOR HOTEL
Sujan Singh Park, Cornwallis Road,
New Delhi-3
Tel: 011-24632600
Fax: 011-24632252

THE CLARIDGES
12, Aurangzeb Road, New Delhi-11
Tel: 011-23010211
Fax:: 011- 23010625
E-mail: info@claridges.com

THE METROPOLITAN HOTEL NIKKO
Bangla Sahib Road, New Delhi-1
Tel: 011-23342000 Fax: 011-23343000
E-mail: nikko@hotelnikkodelhi.com

4 Star Hotels

HOTEL ALKA
16/90 ConnaughtCircus, New Delhi-1
Tel: 011-23344328/23344000
Fax: 011-23742796
E-mail: hotelalka@vsnl.com

HOTEL CITY PARK
K.P.Block, Pitampura, New Delhi-88
Tel:011-27310101-09 Fax: 011-27310110
E-mail: hotelcitypark@vsnl.net

HOTEL DIPLOMAT
9, Sardar Patel Marg, Diplomatic Enclave,
New Delhi-21 Tel: 011-23010204
Fax: 011-23018605
E-mail: diplomat@nda.vsnl.net.in

HOTEL JANPATH
Janpath Road, New Delhi-1
Tel: 011-23340070 Fax: 011-23347083
E-mail: janpath@ndf.vsnl.net.in

HOTEL MARINA
G-59, Connaught Circus, New Delhi-1
Tel: 011-23324658 Fax: 011-23328609
E-mail: hotelmarina@touchtelindia.net

THE CONNAUGHT
37, Shaheed Bhagat Singh Marg,
New Delhi-1 Tel: 011-23364225
Fax: 011-23340757
E-mail: PROMINENT. HOTELS@gems.vsnl.net.in

MAIDENS HOTEL
7, Sham Nath Marg, New Delhi-54
Tel: 011-23975464
Fax:011-23980771/23890595
E-mail: bsparmar@tomdel.com

THE HANS PLAZA
Hansalaya Building, 15, Barakhamba
Road, New Delhi-1
Tel: 011-23316861/23316868
Fax: 011-23314830/23737403
E-mail: hansotel@nde.vsnl.net.in

3 Star Hotels

HOTEL BROADWAY
4/15A, Asaf Ali Road, New Delhi –2
Tel: 011-23273821-25
Fax: 011-23269966
E-mail: broadway@vsnl.net

HOTEL JAGEER PALACE
C-6/1, Mansarover Garden, New Delhi-15
Tel:011-25412939/25420487/55464302/3/4 Fax: 011-25462052
E-mail: info@hoteljageerpalace.com

HOTEL RAJDOOT
Mathura Road, New Delhi-14
Tel: 011-24316666 Fax: 011-24317442

HOTEL SOBTI
2397-98, Hardhian Singh Road, Karol
Bagh, New Delhi-5
TEL: 011-25729030/25729035
Fax: 011-25732028

HOTEL TOURIST DELUXE
7361, Ram Nagar, Qutab Road,
Near New Delhi Railway Station,
Paharganj, New Delhi -55
Tel: 011-23670985
Fax:011-23558416
E-mail: touristdeluxe@vsnl.net

HOTEL VIKRAM
Lajpat Nagar, New Delhi-24
Tel: 011-26436451
Fax:011-26225111/26435657
E-mail: hotelvikram@vsnl.com

JAYPEE GREENS GOLF RESORT
G-Block, Surajpur Kasna Road,
Greater Noida-6
Tel: 0120-4326533/34/36
Fax: 0120-4320150
E-mail: jaypeegreens@yahoo.co.in

NIRULA'S HOTEL
L-Block, Connaught Circus, New Delhi-1
Tel: 011-51517070 Fax: 011-23418957
E-mail: delhihotel@nirulas.com

THE RETREAT MOTEL/RESORT
Alipur, Main G.T. Karnal Road,
Near Palla Mod, Delhi -36
Tel: 011-27207843/27205331
Fax: 011-27708507
E-mail: contact@theretreatresort.com

YORK HOTEL
K-10, Connaught Circus, New Delhi-1
Tel: 011-23415769 Fax: 011-23414419
E-mail: hotelyork@yahoo.co.in

2 Star Hotels
HOTEL ALKA ANNEXE
M-20, Connaught Circus, New Delhi –1
Tel: 011-23416680/23414028
Fax: 011-23742796
E-mail: hotelalka@vsnl.com

HOTEL OASIS
H .D.8, Pitampura, New Delhi-34
Tel: 011-27316869/27311274
Fax: 011-27317765
E-mail: info@oasisgrp.com

HOTEL REGAL
S.P.Mukerjee Marg, New Delhi –6
Tel:011-23976232/23943999
Fax: 011-23915254

HOTEL TOURIST
7361 Ram Nagar, Qutab Road, Near
N.D.Railway Station New Delhi-55
Tel:011-23610334-40
Fax: 011-23559418
E-mail: tourist@schand.com.net.in

JUKASO INN
50 Sunder Nagar, New Delhi-3
Tel: 011- 24350308/9
Fax: 011-24354402
E-mail: jukaso@hotmail.com

TERA HOTEL & RESTAURANT
2802, Bara Bazaar, Kashmiri Gate,
New Delhi -6
Tel: 011-23911532
Fax; 011-23959660

THE MANOR
77 Friends Colony, New Delhi-65
Tel: 011-26925151/26927510
Fax: 011-26922299
E-mail: info@themanordelhi.com

TIVOLI GARDEN RESORT
Khasra No.646-653, Village- Chattarpur,
New Delhi-30
Tel :011-26301111 Fax:011-26303093
E-mail: Tivoli@vsnl.com

Budget Hotels
HOTEL BHAGIRATH PALACE, Chandni
Chowk, Tel:011-23866223

HOTEL FIFTY- FIVE, Connaught Circus,
Tel: 011-23321244/23321278

HOTEL GOLD REGENCY, Paharganj,
Tel:011-23562101/23585559

HOTEL HOST- INN, Connaught Place,
Tel: 011-23310431/23310523

HOTEL NEERU, Daryaganj,
Tel: 011- 23278522/ 23278756

HOTEL SHIELA, 9, Qutab Marg,
Tel: 011-3525603

HOTEL THE NEST, 1! - Qutab Road,
Tel: 011-23526614/23527283

MADHUBAN INN, Greater Kailash,
Tel:011-26219982/26431923

HOTEL BRIGHT, Connaught Circus,
Tel:011-23321433/23329145

HOTEL FLORA, Daryaganj,
Tel:011-23273634-36

HOTEL JEWEL PALCE, Karol Bagh,
Tel:011-25739991/92/93

HOTEL KABEER, Ram Nagar,
Tel: 011-23621301-05

HOTEL NATRAJ, Paharganj,
Tel:011-23522699/23616699/23610099

HOTEL ORCHID, G-4, South Extension
Part-1 , Tel: 011-24643529

HOTEL WOOD INN, Kirti Nagar,
Tel:011- 25438500/25439136

JUKASO INN DOWN TOWN, Connaught
Circus, Tel:011-23415450/51/52/53

PETITE HOTELS, Civil Lines,
Tel:011-55190511/55398200/55909973

PUNJAB HOTEL, Fatehpuri,
Tel:011-23975706

SHIPRA HOTEL, Laxmi Nagar,
Tel:011-22454802/3/4

SODHI LODGE, East of Kailash,
Tel: 011-26432381/26431160/26487869

SOLO VICTORIA, Greater Kailash-1,
Tel:011-26236697/26210732

SOUTH INDIAN HOTEL, Karol Bagh,
Tel:011-51450125/26/27

VIVEK HOTEL, Paharganj,
Tel:011-23512900-02/23521948/23523015

HOTEL PALACE HEIGHTS, Connaught Circus, Tel:011-23411369

INDRAPRASTHA, !9 , Ashok Road ,
Tel : 011-23368383

NEW FRONTIER HOTEL, S.P. Mukerjee Marg, Tel:011-23930795

TOURIST HOLIDAY INN, Jangpura,
Tel:011-24328135/24315750

Other Accommodation

AIRPORT RETIRING ROOMS

DHARAMSHALAS INDIA INTERNATIONAL CENTRE, Lodhi Estate, Tel:011-24619431

RAILWAY RETIRING ROOMS

TOURIST CAMP, Qudsia Gardens,
opp ISBT, Kashmere Gate

TOURIST CAMP, opp Irwin Hospital.
J.L. Nehru Marg

VISHWA YUVAK KENDRA. Circular Road, Chanakyapuri, Tel: 011-23013631

YOUTH HOSTEL, 5 Nyaya Marg, Chanakyapuri

YMCA TOURIST HOSTEL, Jai Singh Road,
Tel:011-311915/312595

YMCA GUEST HOUSE, Jai Singh Road,
Tel:011-3361915

YWCA INTERNATIONAL GUEST HOUSE, Parliament Street, Tel:011-3361561/3361 662/3361740/3361970

YWCA BLUE TRIANGLE FAMILY HOSTEL, Ashoka Road,
Tel: 011-3360133/3361517/3735138

Notes.